W9-COY-544

THE
WORD
MADE
FLESH

OTHER BOOKS BY JOHN BISAGNO

The Power of Positive Praying
The Power of Positive Evangelism
The Power of Positive Living
The Power of Positive Preaching to the Saved
How to Build an Evangelistic Church
The Word of the Lord

THE WORD MADE FLESH

John Bisagno

WORD BOOKS, Publisher
Waco, Texas

THE WORD MADE FLESH
Copyright © 1975 by Word Incorporated,
Waco, Texas.
All rights reserved.
No part of this book may be reproduced in any form,
except for brief quotations in reviews,
without the written permission of the publisher.

Library of Congress catalog card number: 74–27482
Printed in the United States of America

All Scripture quotations, unless otherwise noted, are from the
King James or Authorized Version of the Bible.

Quotations from the Revised Standard Version of the Bible (RSV)
are copyrighted 1946 (renewed 1973), 1956 and © 1971 by the
Division of Christian Education of the National Council of the
Churches of Christ in the U.S.A. and are used by permission.

Quotations from *The New English Bible* (NEB), © The Delegates
of The Oxford University Press and The Syndics of The Cam-
bridge University Press, 1971, 1970, are reprinted by permission.

Quotations from *The Living Bible, Paraphrased,* © 1971 by Tyndale House Publishers, Wheaton, Illinois, are used by permission.

Quotations from J. B. Phillips, *The New Testament in Modern
English,* The Macmillan Company, 1958, are copyright © 1958
by J. B. Phillips.

The poem "What Will You Do with Jesus?" by B. B. McKinney
is copyright 1940 by the Sunday School Board of the Southern
Baptist Convention.

The poem "Down from His Glory" by William E. Booth-Clibborn
is copyright 1921; renewal 1949 by William E. Booth-Clibborn.
Assigned ZHM1. All rights reserved. Used by permission.

To the staff of First Baptist Church, Houston,
whose expertise and commitment to the work of the Lord
make it possible for their pastor to search and to study,
to pray and prepare to preach the Word

Contents

Introduction

The genius of Christianity is the condescension of God acting redemptively through a human body—that body, so perfect, so complete, that in it was contained all of the attributes of a perfect God. Today the church is His body and the composite of all believers form a perfect reflection of Himself to the world. As the church is the visible testimony of Christ now, so for thirty-three years was Jesus Christ, in one person, the tangible testimony of God to the world. He clearly stated, "He that hath seen me hath seen the Father." To know the Christ is to know the Father, and His claim of deity is the touchstone of the Christian gospel. Jesus Christ is God. In Him all the fullness of the Godhead dwells bodily. To believe this is to possess salvation and life. To deny it is the spirit of antichrist and death.

In these pages we shall search from both a theological and devotional perspective the wonder of wonders, the incarnation of God in human form—Jesus Christ, the Savior of mankind, God's only link between the mortal and the immortal.

1. The Living Word

THE PROLOGUE to John's Gospel is considered by some commentators to be the queen of literature. Tennyson wrote, "It is the highest adventure of religious thought attained by the mind of man." St. Augustine reported the reaction of a Platonic philosopher to these first verses of the Gospel—they were "worthy to have been penned in letters of gold." Augustine himself said of the Gospel of John, "Consider then, brethren, if perchance John is not one of those mountains concerning which we sang a little while ago, 'I have lifted up mine eyes to the mountains, from whence come my help.'"

In the beginning was the Word, and the Word was with God, and the Word was God. The same was in the beginning with God. All things were made by him; and without him was not any thing made that was made. In him was life; and the life was the light of men. And the light shineth in darkness; and the darkness comprehended it not.

There was a man sent from God, whose name was John. The same came for a witness, to bear witness of the Light, that all men through him might believe. He was not that Light, but was sent to bear witness of that Light. That was the true Light, which lighteth every man that cometh into the world. He was in the world, and the world was made by him, and the world knew him not. He came unto his own, and his own received him not. But as many as received him, to them gave he power to become the sons of God, even to them that believe on his name. Which were born, not of blood, nor of the will of the flesh, nor of the will of man, but of God. And the Word was made flesh and dwelt among us (and we beheld his glory, the glory as of the only begotten of the Father,) full of grace and truth.

John bare witness of him, and cried, saying, This was he of whom I spake, He that cometh after me is preferred before me; for he was before me. And of his fulness have all we received, and grace for grace. For the law was given by Moses, but grace and truth came by Jesus Christ. No man hath seen God at any time; the only begotten Son, which is in the bosom of the Father, he hath declared him.

The first verse of the prologue raises three questions which must be answered: what is the Word? when was the Word? why is the Word?

What Is the Word?

The Word is Jesus Christ. We are used to calling the Bible "the Word of God," but you will understand that "the Word" here does not mean the Bible. The term is a name for Jesus Christ—the living Word. The Greek word used here is *logos,* which means "the expression of an idea." The living Word of which we read is Jesus Christ. Only in the writings of John is Jesus called "the Word." As the Bible is the written Word, so is Jesus the living Word.

Christians are often accused of having three Gods, but this is a misunderstanding. We have one God whose name is Jehovah. But, this one God chooses to express

Himself in three different forms. For example, H_2O is a chemical formula for the composition of a common substance. This substance comes in three different forms. In liquid form it is called *water*, in solid form *ice*, and in vaporous form *steam*. But, it is always H_2O. Its composition is still the same. Just so, we have one God. When He is in heaven in the business of running His mighty universe, He is in the form of the Father. When He is in the world, revealing Himself in spiritual form, He is the Holy Spirit. And when He steps into the empirical realm, to express God in tangible terms and in human form, He is Jesus Christ. None of these three forms of God are any less of God than the other. There is one difference here where the analogy does not hold up. The same piece of water cannot be at the same time ice and steam as well (although scientists now say that under certain conditions it is possible for water to exist in three states at once). But God is Father, Son, and Spirit always and at all times. He did not cease to be the Father when Jesus Christ lived, nor does Jesus Christ cease being God because the Holy Spirit is active today.

There is no stairstepping of authority in the Trinity. The Son and the Spirit are not subservient or secondary. There is no jealousy. There is no difference of categories. There is but one God who expresses Himself in three forms. Difficult to comprehend? Yes! Theologians have wrestled with the concept of the Trinity through the centuries and have concurred that it is impossible to comprehend completely. In this world we receive sounds and pictures through our radios and television sets without being able to comprehend how they work. Just so, there are truths which we are incapable of comprehending. Once man knew perfectly. But, now distanced from God by sin, he is the victim of partial knowledge and must ask why and how.

One day, when we receive a glorified body like Christ's glorified body, we will have spiritual comprehension. We will have perception that we do not now possess. It is indeed as Socrates said of divine things, "Blessed is the man who accepts them without trying to explain them." It is imperative to understand that Jesus, as the Word, is God. The Apostle John makes it very clear that a false prophet possessing the spirit of antichrist cannot accept that Jesus is the Christ (1 John 2:22–23); Jesus is no ambassador sent from God. He is not a spokesman for God. He is no representative from God. Jesus *is* God!

No founder of any great world religion whom the world has taken seriously ever claimed to be God. Buddha did not. Mohammed did not. They said they were prophets of God. But, Jesus said clearly, "He that hath seen me hath seen the Father," and, "I and my Father are one" (John 14:9; 10:30). Jesus Christ claimed to be God.

When Was the Word?

It is a characteristic of the biblical writers that when something is of particular importance, they repeat it for emphasis. In the first verse of the prologue, John says, "In the beginning was the Word, and the Word was with God and the Word was God." In verse 2 he adds, "The same was in the beginning with God." The Holy Spirit is saying that it is doubly important for us not to miss this important truth. It is the touchstone of the Christian gospel that Jesus is coeternal and coequal with the Father. He did not simply begin to exist on Christmas morning. He always was. "He was in the beginning with God." Hebrews, Colossians, and Revelation make it clear that Jesus is the author, the creator, the force and sustainer of all things (Heb. 1:1–3; Col. 2:9–10; Rev. 4:11). *The Living Bible* puts it this way: "Before anything else existed, there was Christ, with God. He has always been alive and is himself God." *The New English Bible* states: "When all things began, the Word already was. The Word dwelt with God and what God was, the Word was."

The universe and what it contains were created; it had a beginning—the angels, the suns and stars, the planets, the earth. But not so the Word. The Word, Jesus Christ, is eternal. Eternal means more than just everlasting. Christ had no beginning and He has no ending. He is always in the present tense, always the eternal now. God told Moses that His name was "I AM" (Exod. 3:14). Jesus told His Jewish opponents, "Before Abraham was, I am" (John 8:58). In other words, "I am that very I AM." It is not easy to convey by any grammatical vehicle the eternal present tense of the Savior. It is not really correct to say that He always was or always will be, for *was* and *will* denote measurement of time. He is always the I AM in the past tense; he is I AM today; he is I AM tomorrow; He will always be I AM coexistent in time and eternity with the Father.

Why the Word?

We must also answer the question, "Why the Word?" As we have already noted, the word *logos,* which is translated "word," means the expression of an idea or the conveyance of an image. There is no better vehicle with which to convey an idea to make it tangible and comprehensible than by a word. When you hear me speak a word, you understand what is in my mind at that moment, so far as my word is an accurate one.

For several centuries the Old Testament prophets attempted to express the nature of God in their preaching and writing. But then, for about four hundred years the world existed without any kind of clear witness or testimony—there were no prophets to the Jewish people. Then, in the darkness of the first century A.D. the light of God shone. God spoke a word. God expressed Himself to man. The writer to the Hebrews declares, "God, who at sundry times and in divers manners spake in time past unto the fathers by the prophets, hath in these last days spoken to us by his Son" (Heb. 1:1–2). Paul writes to the Colossians that Christ "is the image of the invisible God, the firstborn of every creature" (Col. 1:15).

One cannot touch that which is invisible. And so God, who is spirit, was without expression to man, who is confined to the human limitations of a body. Through Jesus, God expressed who and what He is, what He thinks, what He feels. In Jesus Christ, God, who exists in the spiritual realm, expresses in the physical world, in physical terms what He is like. Jesus Christ is the connecting link between the invisible and the visible, between the spiritual world and the physical, between the natural and the divine. Just as the Bible is the written Word of God, so Jesus is the Word acted out, lived out, personified. The Bible is God on paper. Jesus is God in a person. The Bible is the written Word. Jesus is the living Word. The Bible is God in a book. Jesus is God in a body. The Bible is God on a leaf. Jesus is God in a life.

God, who has spoken to us by His voice, by the prophets, by nature, by the Spirit, by direct revelation, has in these last days spoken to us by His Son, Jesus, the living Word. The Book of Genesis records the original sin of man. After Adam sinned, the Scripture writer affirms that Adam heard the voice of God walking in the garden. According to the Hebrew construction of this sentence, a mysterious truth is suggested. It is not that Adam heard the voice of God while he was walking, but Adam heard the voice of God walking. Jesus is the voice of God. He is the Alpha and the Omega, the whole Greek alphabet. He is everything God has to say about Himself. That voice, that living Word, Christ Himself came to Adam in the garden.

The Book of Daniel tells us the story of Shadrach, Meshach, and Abednego who were thrust into the fiery furnace for their fidelity to Jehovah. But when the door of the furnace was opened, the guards were amazed to see a fourth person in the fire, like unto the Son of God. Jesus was there as well. Every prenativity visit of God to man was in the person of Jesus Christ. When Daniel was thrown into the lion's den, someone closed the jaws of the lions and he survived. Jesus was in the lion's den with Daniel.

When the Old Testament saints died looking into the face of God, when the apostles sealed their testimony in blood as Stephen at martyrdom, they all saw the welcoming face of Jesus. And, when we shall see God face to face, when we shall see Him high and holy, lifted up and His glory filling heaven, we will see His exalted Son, Jesus, the Lamb of God.

The Bible is a book about Jesus Christ. He is the heart and center of its meaning and the hope of its promise.

The Holy Spirit ransacked creation to describe Him. He went to the animal kingdom and called Him the Lion of the tribe of Judah and the Lamb of God. He went to the kingdom of astronomy and called Him the bright and morning star and the Sun of righteousness. He went to the mineral kingdom and called Him the Water of Life and the pearl of great price. And to the kingdom of botany where He is described as the rose of Sharon and the lily of the valleys.

Jesus Christ is the Alphabet of God: the Alpha; the bread of life; the Christ; the Deliverer; the everlasting Father; Faithful and True; the gift of God; the Healer; Immanuel; the Judge of quick and dead; the King of kings; the Lord of lords; the Messiah; the name above every name; the Omnipotent God; our passover (lamb); the quickener from the dead; the Resurrection; the Savior of the world; the Truth; the unspeakable gift; the vine; the Way; the express image of God; yesterday, today, and forever the same; Zion's hope.

Jesus Christ is God!

At the climax of the battle for Scotland, Robert Bruce was killed. The Scottish soldiers turned in fear and began to retreat. One brave soldier, seeing the body of his hero on the ground, raced forward and cut out the heart of Robert Bruce with his sword. With blood dripping from his hand, he held it high in the face of oncoming British troops and cried, "There goes the heart of Bruce. Who follows after?" In one triumphant moment, the Scottish armies turned, flinging themselves against the fury of enemy swords, and followed the heart of Bruce. Scotland was saved.

One day, two thousand years ago, because God so loved the world, He held His own heart high, dripping with blood on an old rugged cross from the body of His own Son. Looking at this action we may say "Here is how God loves. Here is the heart of God in a man, Jesus Christ. Who will follow after him?"

2. The Creator

"All things were made by him; and without him was not any thing made that was made" (John 1:3).

As A JEW addressing Jews, the importance of John's words cannot be overstated. To the Jew, words were powerful. A word was a unit charged with electrifying life, truth, and power. One Hebrew word could convey as much meaning as entire sentences today. The Greek language, however, contains in excess of twenty thousand words and has more parts of speech than the average English-speaking person can imagine. So, when Jesus was presented to the world as "the Word," the title was filled with great meaning—the Word of God, the vocabulary of God, the voice of God.

Having introduced Jesus as the Word, John the great philosopher-theologian makes a dynamic assertion. Not only does John declare that Jesus existed before all things, but now he adds that He *created all things*. And for emphasis he states it in both the negative and positive form: "All things were made by him; and without him was not any thing made that was made."

The New English Bible states, "The Word, then, was with God at the beginning, and through him all things came to be; no single thing was created without him." Colossians 1:16–17 states, "For by him were all things created, that are in heaven, and that are in earth, visible and invisible, whether they be thrones, or dominions, or principalities, or powers: all things were created by him, and for him: and he is before all things, and by him all things consist." "By him all things consist"—literally, by Him all things hold together. All things in eternity, heaven, and earth, and society are held together by Jesus. He is society's glue. He is the end of the philosopher's search for ultimate truth.

In considering Christ's role in creation, three questions must be answered: What did He make? How did He make them? Why did He make them?

What Did He Make?

Paul divides creation into two categories—things that are made in heaven and things that are made in earth. In the earth, he defines two categories—invisible and visible. The invisible things are again subcategorized.

Paul's experience of being caught up into the third heaven has caused our Mormon friends to suggest that heaven is divided into three spiritual states. In fact, however, the three heavens to which the Scriptures allude are first, the heavens that immediately surround us containing the air we breathe and where the birds fly. Second is outer space where the astronauts soar and where the planets hang. The third heaven is the home of God. In all the heavens, Jesus as Creator and living Word is Lord. It was He who said, "Let there be light," and there was light. For, He Himself is the Light of the world—the true light, the light of every man who comes into the world. In the second heaven, the "heavens declare the glory of God; and the firmament sheweth his handywork" (Ps. 19:1). The celestial constellations, the billions of galaxies that look like a white, misty haze across the sky—they, too, are His creations and His glory. And in the eternal heaven there is neither sun by day nor moon by night, for "the Lamb is the light" (Rev. 21:23).

The earth is the second of Paul's categories of creation, and here the Creator, the Savior, is Lord also. It was He who covered the earth with a carpet of grass and tacked it down with the beautiful flowers. It was He who piled up the mountains and scooped out the valleys. It was He who wove a beautiful robe of color and threw it about the shoulders of the dying storm and called it the rainbow.

It was He who made the invisible things as well—the sovereignty, the powers, the dominions, the principalities—He holds them all in the palm of His hand. Don't think for one minute that this old world is out of control. The Bible says it is God who sets up one king and takes down another (Dan. 2:21). "The powers that be are ordained of God" (Rom. 13:1). Though this world is out of balance with itself, and can only be ultimately reconciled to itself as it is reconciled to God, God is even now holding it together, for God was in Christ reconciling the world unto Himself. The world is never left to blind chance. Jesus has the whole wide world in His hand. He made all things that are in heaven and in earth, visible and invisible.

How Did God Make Them?

When we consider the question of how God created the universe, we should note that the ten steps listed in the order of creation in Genesis are the exact ten steps by which scientists now agree that life was created on earth and in their proper order. When the writer of Genesis tells us, "In the beginning God created the heaven and the earth" (Gen. 1:1), he uses a plural word for God—*elohim*—giving us a hint of the Trinity at work. Perhaps it was the Father's idea, the Spirit's power, and the Son's creativity which cooperated to bring the world into existence. The New Testament tells us—as we see in our verse in John, and in other places—that the Father gave the Son the privilege of creating a world that would glorify and honor Him.

Precisely how He created the world we do not know. But the Genesis writer gives us insight into the strong probability of instantaneous creation. "Let there be light. . . . Let the waters under the heaven be gathered together. . . . Let the earth bring forth grass" (Gen. 1:3, 9, 11). And so it appears that it was by the word of His mouth that creation occurred. Often people ask the question, "If there is not life on other planets, why did God go to the trouble to create them?" Well, the truth is that it was no trouble, for He simply said, "Let it be" and it was! By the word of His mouth He created the world.

Why Did God Create?

The third question is "Why did He do it?" Why did God make this world anyway? What sense is there behind it all? The answer is a simple one. He made the world for His own glory. He made it a perfect paradise upon which man could live and work and produce children also made in the image of God. But man failed the test God set him and sinned, so that God's image in him was defaced—though not lost. So now it is by the redeeming power of Christ that God will bring many children to adoption. The earth was to become filled with children of God reproduced in His wonderful image, that heaven might be filled with billions and billions like Jesus Christ. The Apostle John says in his first letter: "In this was manifested the love of God toward us, because that God sent his only begotten Son into the world, that we might live through him. Herein is love, not that we loved God, but that he loved us, and sent his Son to be the propitiation for our sins. Beloved, if God so loved us, we ought also to love one another" (1 John 4:9–11).

So, we see that it was for His glory, joy, and pleasure that the world was created. Like a father lavishing gifts upon his son, God created the world for the glory of Christ that men might be transformed and glorified into His perfect image. The grand and glorious ultimate end of man, then, is to have fellowship and relationship with God and to be like Him. Jesus made it very clear on the Sermon on the Mount that He had come to teach men how to be happy . . . happy in union and fellowship with Him. "Blessed"—that is, happy—"are the pure in heart: for they shall see God" (Matt. 5:8). But man has become unhappy, and the source of his unhappiness is sin, because sin separates man from God, who is the source of happiness.

The question is often asked if life exists on other planets. One thing is clear. If it is, it is not a higher type of life than ours, for we are made in the image of God, and you just cannot do any better than that! It was not to Mars or Venus, but to Earth that God came to create His creature in His own image. Jesus created the earth, placed men on the earth to love Him and have fellowship with Him and to reproduce his own kind. But when man sinned the story did not end. "For God so loved the world, that he gave his only begotten Son." Yes, the Creator became the Savior and came to finish the plan by which heaven could be populated with many glorified sons like the Son of God. "The earth is the Lord's, and the fulness thereof" (Ps. 24:1), and the plan of God in creation is to bring many sons unto adoption.

3. The Life

"In him was life; and the life was the light of men"
(John 1:4).

THE APOSTLE JOHN sums up the purpose of his Gospel
by stating, "These [things] are written that you may
believe that Jesus is the Christ, the Son of God, and that
believing you may have life in his name" (John 20:31,
RSV). The twin themes of John's writings are *life* and
light. Thirty times he uses the word *light*. Fifty-nine
times he uses the word *life*. Verse 4 of the prologue introduces both themes: "In him was life; and the life was
the light of men."

First of all, life is to be found exclusively in Jesus
Christ. It is not an attribute of His, it is not a gift, it is
not merely offered by Him. Life is in Him! He is life.
Life is to be found only in Christ.

Throughout the centuries, men have tried to find the
essence and meaning of life. Philosophers have joined
the search, and come to the conclusion that the meaning
of life cannot be found; philosophy can only give a person the tools to make his own search. But the meaning of
life is not to be found by the scientists, the geologists, or
the philosophers, for it lies in the area of the super-

natural. It is a spiritual matter. The meaning of life is in Jesus Christ. He is its crux and being, its origin and consummation.

"I thought that in my own striving for perfection I could find the meaning of life," is one man's testimony. "I tried in my own righteousness. I found that I did what I would not, and that in striving to find holiness and happiness, I became miserable to the point of near insanity. And then I understood for the first time those words, 'In Him was life.' "

Those who seek to find salvation through works have sought in vain. In Christ is life. Some believe that to follow the teachings of Christ—His precepts and ethics —is to have life. Not so. *In* Him is life. Salvation is in a man. Life is in a person. So few comprehend that. That is why when people join our church I never ask them, "Do you accept me or my church or its teaching?" Rather, I ask "Do you accept Christ?" Life is to be found in a person.

Second, if it is true that life is to be found exclusively in Jesus Christ, then it follows that apart from Him there is only death. Romans 6:23 states that the wages— the fruition, the result—of sin, that is, of life lived in separation from Jesus Christ, is death. One of the most common problems college students experience in their witnessing to their friends is that they hear the answer, "I do not have Christ, yet I am still very happy." This is like saying, "I'm happy driving a Model A." Model A's are all right until one discovers Cadillacs. Hot dogs may be very tasty to the man who has never enjoyed a T-bone steak. Admittedly, there is a limited degree of happiness to be found apart from Jesus Christ. But one cannot know ultimate happiness until he comes into relationship with Him and experiences what he has never known before.

Life without Christ is really no life at all. It is pulse without purpose, heart without happiness, existence without eternity, life without living. It is a pigmy that could be a giant, a boy that could be a man, a nobody that could be a somebody. It is like playing on forty strings of a thousand-string harp. Like dabbling on four or five notes of a four- or five-manual organ. Life without Jesus is no life at all. No wonder Will L. Thompson wrote,

> Jesus is all the world to me,
> My life, my joy, my all.

Third, the means through which we may have this life is faith. It is offered exclusively upon the basis of faith. It is ours for the believing. John 3:36 states, "He that believeth on the Son hath . . . life." Jesus adds, "I am come that they might have life and that they might have it more abundantly" (John 10:10). Notice that He wants us to have life. Not only is He the life, but He offers to give that life to us.

The mighty eighth chapter of Romans begins with the powerful truth, "There is therefore now no condemnation to them which are in Christ Jesus." There is no reason to live a second-rate kind of spiritual life, clothed in religiosity, but dead within. Jesus Christ offers us abundant life. A vibrant, dynamic, pulsating kind of life is promised to those who are in Him.

It is possible to be a bantam Baptist, a crippled Catholic or a dead Disciple, a puny Presbyterian, a pitiful Pentecostal, or a midget Methodist. It is possible to be religious but lost. It is possible to be *around* the things of Christ and yet not be *in* Christ. By faith we are grafted into oneness with Him. As a branch has no potential for life except as it stays connected to the vine, just so, spiritually dead men cannot live except as they are engrafted by faith into the living Word. "Christ liveth in me" was the way Paul put it. "I live by the faith of the Son of God" (Gal. 2:20). It is the exchanged life—my sinful self in exchange for His glorious self. It is exchanging all that I am for all that He is and letting Him live in and through me!

Years ago a great Mexican emperor was converted to faith in Christ. Though he had had everything, somehow he had nothing and was never really a king on the inside. After he met the Savior, he wrote in beautiful poetic form of his conversion,

> Once I was a spark, Lord,
> But you have made me a fire.
> Once I was but a string,
> And now I am a lyre.
> Once I was but a drop,
> Now I am a fountain.
> Once I was a hill,
> But now I am a mountain.
> Once I was a link,
> But now I am a chain.
> Once I was a sprinkle,
> But now I am a rain.
> Once I was fettered,
> But now I can sing.
> Once a beggar,
> But now I am a king.

4. The Light Shines

"And the light shineth in darkness; and the darkness comprehended it not" (John 1:5).

As THE PHRASES "kingdom of light" and "the light of the world" always speak of Christ and His kingdom, so "the darkness" always refers to Satan's kingdom of death and sin.

A publication recently crossed my desk entitled *The Process*. It is the official magazine of a new and weird cult. The simple thesis of the cult is that because Christ said, "Love your enemies," and Satan was His enemy, Jesus, therefore, loved Satan and is in collusion with him. Not so! Satan's kingdom of darkness and Christ's kingdom of light are ever in mortal conflict. Jesus said, "Every kingdom divided against itself is brought to desolation; and every city or house divided against itself shall not stand: and if Satan cast out Satan, he is divided against himself; how shall then his kingdom stand?" (Matt. 12:25–26).

Paul scolds the Corinthian church for their erroneous attempt to reconcile the kingdom of darkness and the kingdom of light. "Be ye not unequally yoked together with unbelievers: for what fellowship hath righteousness with unrighteousness? and what communion hath light with darkness? and what concord hath Christ with Belial? or what part hath he that believeth with an infidel?" (2 Cor. 6:14–15). Wisely has Socrates said, "Let us each turn from every other pursuit and give ourselves to this one end; that we should know and discern between good and evil."

The word *comprehend* in the King James Version of this verse is a poor translation. A more realistic translation for the twentieth century is "overcome." "And the light shined in darkness and the darkness overcame it not"—the darkness could not put it out, could not defeat it. The kingdom of darkness can never tear down the kingdom of light, though it has tried through the centuries to snuff it out. It tried in the second millennium before Christ, when Joseph's brothers sold him into Egyptian captivity. In an Egyptian prison it seemed that the light of goodness would go out and evil would prevail. Later, Joseph looked back on the experience and said, "You meant evil against me; but God meant it for good" (Gen. 50: 20, rsv).

In describing the near end of Christianity at its very inception, Paul recounts the events of the gospel with a dead Christ in a tomb and pauses . . . "But God raised him from the dead" (Acts 13:30). In writing to the Ephesians, Paul recounts the awfulness and power of sin. The Ephesians "were dead in trespasses and sins: wherein in time past ye walked according to the course of this world, according to the prince of the power of the air, the spirit that now worketh in the children of disobedience." Then he goes on to describe the awfulness of sinful nature: "Among whom we all had our conversation in times past in the lusts of our flesh, fulfilling the desires of the flesh and of the mind; and were by nature the children of wrath, even as others." But sin did not have the last word. "But God, who is rich in mercy, for his great love wherewith he loved us, even when we were dead in sins, hath quickened us together with Christ, (by grace ye are saved)" (Eph. 2:1–5).

Just before the birth of the Savior, the kingdom of darkness entered the heart of Caesar Augustus and he sent out a decree that all the world be taxed. Jesus, in the body of Mary his mother, was jostled over the seventy-five miles of rough mountain roads and cobblestone streets that connected Nazareth to Bethlehem. By every rule of the book He should have been born sick or injured or dead. But he wasn't. God prepared a cradle in a stable. In a Palestinian hillside Jesus Christ was born, and the Light of the world shone more brightly than ever before.

Early in the fourth century, Constantine, riding into battle against a rival claimant to the throne of the Roman Empire, saw a cross of light in the heavens and heard a voice saying, "In this sign conquer." Constantine adopted the cross as his standard and won the battle. Eventually he became a Christian, and by the end of his reign, Christianity was practically the religion of the Empire.

During the Dark Ages the priests turned to gross immorality and the church sank to despotic depths. When it seemed that the Light would go out again Wycliff and the Lollards translated the Bible into idiomatic English and taught it to the common people during the fourteenth century. At the same time John Hus was preaching the true gospel in Bohemia (modern Hungary) and Savonarola was preaching righteous living in Italy. God does not leave Himself without a witness. In the sixteenth century in Germany, Martin Luther burst upon the scene, and Calvin and Zwingli followed in Switzerland. Tyndale worked in England. The kingdom of darkness was shaken and the Light again shone clearly in the world.

Shortly after the dawn of the twentieth century, communism with its atheistic militancy was born. Following Karl Marx, communism vowed to "obliterate the myth of God from the minds of men forever." Yet, today there are few places in the world where the Christian gospel is loved with a deeper intensity than in the hearts of many secret believers in the Soviet Union's underground church.

"The light still shines in the darkness, and the darkness has never put it out" (John 1:5, Phillips). The enemies of God have come and gone and are buried beneath the shifting sands of the shores of a hundred civilizations, but the Galilean lives on! Hallelujah! In spite of discouragement and despair, in spite of temporary reversals, the name of Jesus Christ and those who love Him shall ultimately prevail. His will shall be done. The darkness will not put out His glorious light. The kingdoms of this world will become the kingdoms of our God and of His Son. Paul reminds us that in this dark world we also shine as lights. And, if the light of the world is to overcome, then we are to overcome. J. Wilbur Chapman has said it so beautifully:

> One day when heaven was filled with His praises,
> One day when sin was as black as could be,
> Jesus came forth to be born of a virgin—
> Dwelt among men, my Redeemer is He!
>
> Living He loved me, dying He saved me,
> Buried He carried my sins far away.

Rising He justified freely forever,
Some day He's coming—oh, glorious day!

In the fourth century A.D., Julian, a successor to Constantine, ruler of the Roman Empire and nominal Christian, denounced his faith in Christ. The early church fathers said that he brought more dishonor on the name of Christ than any man that lived in their time, and gave him the name "the Apostate." Julian went to war against the cause of Christ and tried to restore pagan idolatry as the religion of the Roman Empire and by doing so to eradicate Christianity. At the peak of the battle in which he was defeated, with broken body and an emaciated face, bloody hand clenched toward heaven, Julian cried in agony and death, "Galilean, thou hast conquered."

Conquer He does and conquer He shall.

Ye trembling saint, fresh courage take,
The right shall yet prevail.
The rebellious world shall bow and cry,
All hail! All hail!

To God be the glory! The light shines in the darkness. And the darkness cannot put it out.

5. The Darkness

"And the light shineth in darkness; and the darkness comprehended it not" (John 1:5).

IT IS IMPOSSIBLE to have a full appreciation of John's dynamic statement, "The light shineth in darkness," until we understand the awesomeness and awfulness of that darkness.

When we search the record books of history we find amazing concepts of that darkness have been held by men. To the Greek, learned and educated, the darkness was a place of awful and chaotic nothingness. It was a waste, a vaporous gaseous void. Such was their concept of spiritual darkness. To the superstitious masses on the street, the darkness spoke of a place where the evil spirits lived, a kind of spooky demonic world filled with creeping and crawling things.

The Egyptian concept of eternal darkness was of a place separate from all human contact and goodness. In a special ceremony of investitured immortality, the Egyptians placed a pole with a ring and a spur at the top into the nostrils of the pharaoh, investing him with immortality to enable him to fight the awful powers of darkness that were sure to engulf him in the world of the dead beyond the grave.

The early Jewish theologians strained every mental process to describe the awful darkness before the spirit of light re-created the world. The Hittites, the Arabs, the Jews, the Babylonians, the Amorites all conceived of darkness as a dismal, bottomless pit. Each layer was like a floating black cloud, blown by the wind. The deeper one went, the heavier and more tangible the clouds became, until ultimately there was such an intensity about them that they actually became personality. Eventually they gave it the form and personality of a female goddess, the goddess of darkness. And they created a god of the upper world, a god of light to send down and slay the goddess of darkness.

Paul speaks of men so blinded by evil that they pervert the natural acts of life to such an extent that their minds are darkened and therefore "God gave them up" (Rom. 1:24, 26, 28). Jesus speaks of the end of the world and the coming of great tribulation when the sun will "be darkened, and the moon shall not give her light, and the stars shall fall from heaven, and the powers of the heavens shall be shaken" (Matt. 24:29). He also speaks of judgment where men shall be cast into outer darkness and there shall be weeping and wailing and gnashing of teeth (Matt. 22:13; 25:30). How awful is this world of moral evil and unspeakable darkness, this world that man has created by his sin.

The word *comprehended,* as we have seen, is better translated as "overcame." It is the Greek word *katalambano* meaning literally "to take down"—in other words, to seize, win, make one's own. It carries with it the idea of the capture of a great city. In olden times, a city's walls not only protected it but were the symbol of its authority and power. After capturing and defeating a city, an enemy might prolong the agony and humiliation of defeat by taking down the walls a brick at a time and laying them side by side on the ground in the eyes of the people. The implication is that Satan not only hates the Christian and hates God and the kingdom of light, but that if possible, he would rub our noses in the humiliation of our sin. But, thanks be unto God, who has translated us from darkness into the kingdom of light, the kingdom of His dear Son. Satan can never make the believer his own. He can never take him down and embarrass him in the humiliation of his defeat.

It is said that when the first gas lights were brought to the crime-ridden suburbs of Chicago in the twenties, the crime rate was cut by 1,000 percent. One little boy, seeing an old lamplighter hobbling from pole to pole in the darkness, asked his father what he was doing. "Ah, son," he said, "he is just punching holes in the darkness." Just so, we as witnesses for Christ in the light of the world are punching holes in the kingdom of darkness. We may never win the world single-handedly to faith in Christ, but there is much that we can do. Here and there one heart can be touched. Here and there we can punch some holes in the darkness.

Never despair, never fear, Christian, you who are the light of the world. We are in an eternal conflict with the kingdom of darkness. Under the banner of our Christ in His glorious kingdom of light we shall never fail. We shall prevail. We shall be victorious.

"And the light shineth in darkness; and the darkness comprehended it not."

6. The Messenger

"There was a man sent from God whose name was John" (John 1:6).

IN YOUR IMAGINATION come with me to the banks of the Jordan, that river that looms so large in Jewish history. There stands a mighty crowd listening to a rough and rugged country preacher. His preaching has emptied the cities—everyone wants to hear what he has to say. In thundering tones he speaks of the judgment of God and demands repentance in the name of heaven.

At first the people are astonished. Are they not the seed of Abraham? Are they not the chosen people of God? Do they not attend weekly synagogue and temple worship? Are they not the most ardent observers of the feast days? What need have they of repentance? But the preacher continues with staccato precision, naming their sins not only nationally, but individually and personally. And they began to see themselves as God sees them. One by one they crowd closer. Struck with conviction, they fall to their knees and confess their sins. Immediately they are baptized in the River Jordan, acknowledging their repentance toward God.

Who is this mighty preacher? Who is this that, after

four hundred years of darkness, dawns on the scene of history as the prophetic voice of a God who has not spoken for centuries? He is one born fulfilling Malachi's prophecy: "Behold, I will send you Elijah the prophet before the coming of the great and dreadful day of the Lord: and he shall turn the heart of the fathers to the children" (Mal. 4:5–6; Matt. 11:11–14). He was the "voice of him that crieth in the wilderness, Prepare ye the way of the Lord," as foretold by the prophet Isaiah (Isa. 40:3). He is John the Baptist, a preacher's son, the herald of God to announce the imminent coming of the long-awaited Messiah.

We have seen that God has given the world life, and has given it light to know how to use the life. Here we have the witness to know about the light. Let us now consider the witness.

First, it is important to note that the man is named. He is not just another man, not just a nobody who has passed across the scene of life and dropped into the realm of the unknown. He is important. He has made the book. He is named. Why? Because he is a witness. And though he might not be important in the eyes of many worldly people, he is of great importance to God. Important because the totality of his being is molded by the will of God. You see it in his dress. You see it in his eyes. You hear it in his voice. It is in his diet, his habitat, the totality of the man's existence. He is a man preoccupied, not with creating a place in history for himself, but with the will of God and preparing the way of the Christ, the Messiah. Later he said of Christ, "He must increase, but I must decrease" (John 3:30).

If John had been untrue to his responsibility to witness to the Christ, that all men through Him might believe, would any other men have been saved? Had God planned another witness, another way, another forerunner? We don't know the answer, but the question should make us stop and think, lest we thwart the will of God by failing to be His instruments.

John was a very special man. He was named of God and called by our Lord the greatest man ever born of women because of his fidelity to God and His will (Matt. 11:11). The selection of a name for a Jewish child was a very important and significant matter. Names were not picked at random. A person was not necessarily named after an ancestor. A name was picked to signify character or qualities, and often proved to be both prophetic of and synonymous with a person's character and task. The name *John* signifies "grace of Jehovah," or "to whom the Lord is gracious"—that is, beloved of God. It has often been true that Johns were especially loved—Jonathan, David's friend; John, the beloved apostle; John Mark; John Hus; John Calvin and John Wesley.

Why is John the Baptist beloved of God? Why is he special to God? Because here is a man true to his task, completely faithful as a witness to the Light of the world.

What are the characteristics about John which caused our Lord Jesus to say, "Among those born of women there has risen no one greater" (Matt. 11:11, RSV)? I would suggest to you, for one thing, that he was a timely man. He was born in God's plan in the fullness of time; he was God's man in God's place at God's time. There is always a sense of holy urgency about the man that God uses. It is always now with him! The present matters above everything else. Jesus said that the law and the prophets were until John (Luke 16:16). John was unique. John was pivotal. He was the last prophet. He was the immediate forerunner of the kingdom of God—the introducer of the Messiah. Therefore, he had to be precisely God's man in God's time. There was an overriding sense of urgency about John . . . *he must be on time for God.*

John was "sent from God." That is basically the meaning of the word *apostle*—"sent one." If we are to be God's servants, we must respond where and when we are sent. The world may never know how much has been lost because God's servants were not on time!

Second, John the Baptist was a great man because he was a humble man. The word *was* in the sentence, "There was a man," is the Greek *egeneto* meaning, "became," that is, "having derived being." The word used in the first sentence of the prologue, "In the beginning *was* the Word," is *hēn* meaning "innate or inherent being." There was no question in John's mind that his Lord was greater than he, that Christ's being was innate and John's was derived from Him, and that as a witness sent from God, he must be God's tool, God's witness on time.

When the Pharisees asked John if he were Elijah raised from the dead, he said, "I am not" (John 1:21). You must understand that I am nothing and He is everything. I am but a voice crying in the wilderness. He who comes after me is preferred before me. It is He whose shoelaces I am not worthy to fasten. He was before me and is preferred before me in all things. (Cf. John 1:23–30).

When Leonardo da Vinci was painting that great picture of the Last Supper, he showed it to an artist friend for his opinion. "What a lovely cup in the Master's hand," responded his friend. Immediately da Vinci stroked out the cup and painted it again in less ornate fashion saying, "I will have nothing in this picture that distracts from the face of Jesus Christ." Just so, must we say with John, "He must increase, but I must decrease" (John 3:30). John the Baptist was a great man because he was a humble man.

Third, he was a great man because he was a stable man. "What went ye out into the wilderness to see?" asked Christ. A reed shaking in the wind, a fancy dan, a courtier in a king's court? Oh, no! Not John. He was faithful, confident, not swayed by material possessions, and steadfast unto death.

But, fourth and most important of all, he was a great man because he was faithful to a great purpose. He was a faithful witness and a faithful message-bearer. The Greek god, Mercury, was thought to be a winged-footed messenger, soaring across the heavens and bringing messages from God to men. Before the battle of Marathon between the Greeks and the Persians, one of the fifteen great battles of history, a runner named Pheidippides ran 150 miles to Sparta to warn them to prepare for the imminent invasion of the Persians and to ask for help. After the battle an unnamed hero called simply "The Greek" ran 26 miles to Athens to tell his fellow citizens that the Greeks had defeated the Persians. Paul Revere became an American hero for his ride from Boston to Lexington with the message that the British were coming. But no man ever had a more awesome responsibility than John the Baptist as a message-bearer of the news of the impending kingdom of heaven. No angel could have done the job, for angels do not know the joy of salvation! God does not primarily use churches or instruments or music or causes or organizations. He uses people! He uses men and women! There was a man of God whose name was John. It is always God's way to use an individual. And if this world, bound in the darkness of sin, will ever be saved, it will be because we will be willing witnesses to the Light of the world.

Legend has it that God considered sending the angels to bear the good news of redemption in Christ, but decided upon men. His first messenger asked Him a question: "Lord, what if I fail? What will you do? Will you send an angel in my place? Will you arrange the message of God's love in the heavenly constellations so that men can read it in the skies? What if I fail? Will you invent some other method by which the good news of the Light of the world can be spread?" In the legend, God says to the witness, "Redeemed sinner, prepare your heart. Empty yourself and be filled with me. Go and do your very best. But remember, if you fail, I have no other way!"

I pray that we might be His faithful witnesses, that we might hear His "Well done," so that it might be recorded of us as John records in beautiful simplicity of John the Baptist: He was "a man sent from God," who came "to bear witness of the Light."

7. Witness to the Light

"There was a man sent from God, whose name was John. The same came for a witness, to bear witness of the Light, that all men through him might believe" (John 1:6–7).

GOD HAS ALWAYS had a witness in the world. Sometimes it is the arching heavens above—"The heavens declare the glory of God" (Ps. 19:1). Sometimes it is a witness of the conscience. At times nature witnesses to God's power and presence (Ps. 8:1). At times God Himself is His own witness.

Joshua built a monument of rock beneath the mighty oaks at Shechem, saying, "This . . . shall be a witness unto us" (Josh. 24:27). The ark of the testimony was a witness to God's revelation and presence with His people (Exod. 25:21–22). The law of the testimony, the tabernacle of the testimony were all witnesses to God.

But there came a time when the world had no new, active witness. For nearly four hundred years God was silent. During this time Zoroastrianism had gripped the world and people believed that the god of darkness and the god of light wrestled daily for control of the destinies of man. If a man died on the day that the god of darkness won, it was believed that he was cast forever into the bottomless pit of dark and endless hopelessness. Into that world came John the Baptist, the last of the Old Testament prophets.

God had given the world life, and light on the meaning of life, and now He sends His witness to point men to the Light. The word *witness* is a legal term which speaks volumes of the power of the spoken word . . . the authority of the word declared. In John's day, a man's word was his bond. When one spoke a word about another, that word was to be true. To speak a lie was to be cursed, for a man's witness, his word, carried with it the weight of his integrity. The liar was the most hated man in the Zoroastrian world. A man who would lie about anything was a man who would lie about everything.

John came as a man who spoke the truth—truth about the witness of the Light on the meaning of life. When he announced that men were to repent because the kingdom of God was at hand, it struck powerful conviction into the hearts of his hearers, because a fellow Jew would not lie. To say, "Damn you," "To hell with you," was to risk death, because the power of that curse was irrevocable due to the power of the spoken word. Just so, the word of the prophet, the positive word of the impending kingdom of heaven was forcefully received by the Baptist's hearers.

As any good lawyer will attempt to prove in a court of law, the character of the witness and the quality of his testimony stand and fall together. John was an impeccable witness. He deprived himself of social prominence and ordinary comforts to give himself to his task. As John the beloved apostle records, John the Baptist was not the Light, but simply came as a witness to the Light that all

men through him might believe (John 1:7). Christ was
the Light; John was the witness to the Light. Christ's
being was inherent. John's was derived. Christ always
was. John came to be. Christ was God. John was sent
from God. Christ was the object of the witness. John was
the vehicle of the witness. John fully understood that if
he failed to bear a powerful witness that would stick in
the hearts of men, they would not believe. How many of
us who are his spiritual grandchildren would be lost had
he failed in his task?

In his letter to the Romans, Paul writes that "whosoever shall call upon the name of the Lord shall be saved"
(Rom. 10:13). But, he adds quickly, how are they going
to "call on him in whom they have not believed? And
how shall they believe in him of whom they have not
heard?" (Rom. 10:14). In other words, a witness is
needed so that people may hear.

Notice that John the apostle says that the word of the
witness is to *all* men. John came to bear witness to the
Light that all men might believe. This is easy for us to
forget. In his letter to Jewish Christians, James the
brother of Jesus warns against class distinctions. It is
wrong, he says, if a man comes into your church wearing
fine, expensive clothing, and you offer him the finest
seat, and at the same time you offer the poor man in
shabby clothes the back seat. We are to be all things to
all men so that by all means we may win some (1 Cor.
9:22). It might take a grand philharmonic to win some
or a converted western singer to win someone else; a
beautiful cathedral to attract some or an evangelistic tent
down in a poverty area to attract some others. But the
church must be true to the commitment that is ours—to
all men.

In a sense, it is strange that the Light would need a witness, for light is a witness to itself. By its very nature, light illuminates, attracts, gives awareness. So, it is not the Light that needs the witness. It is people who need the witness. What kind of people? People blinded by sin. Those who are spiritually dead have no eyes for the things of God. They have physical eyes, but they are spiritually blind. They have physical ears but they do not hear.

Every day such individuals come under the influence of amazing grace, and yet do not have the slightest idea what they hear. It is the Christian's task to interpret, to direct, to explain, to witness to those in darkness as to the meaning of the Light. In the very strictest sense, we are not really soul-winners as much as we are witnesses. Indeed, it is true that a successful witnessing experience is sharing Christ in the power of the Holy Spirit and leaving the results to God. The results are His, but the witness is ours. Only the Holy Spirit can illuminate the witness, scatter spiritual darkness and reveal the Light. Billy Graham says, "I am like a Western Union boy delivering the message. What men do with that message is between them and God." That is very true. But we must be careful to be faithful Western Union boys, giving a faithful witness to the meaning of the Light of the world.

Why are we to be witnesses to the Light? That all men might believe. Somehow, at this point, it seems as though God bares His heart to plead for the salvation of all men as He says, "I want all men to hear the witness to the Light. I want all men to have the life that I offer in Christ." John the Baptist is the first of a long line of witnesses through whom God's message has been shouted to the world. "Repent, go ahead and get ready now. The kingdom is coming. The Messiah is at hand. Now is the accepted time. Today is the day of salvation. Now is the time for missionary advance and for evangelical witness." For as John must be faithful to his task as a witness that we might believe through him, just so, we must be faithful that yet unborn generations might believe through us.

When the first transoceanic broadcast took place, the king of England prepared to speak to millions of Americans. Seconds before the broadcast began, it is said that the chief engineer noticed that the wires had been short-circuited, which meant that the message could not be broadcast. Grasping the wires by either end he held them with his two hands and allowed the message to flow to the waiting world through his body. Like that engineer, we are to be instruments in God's hands, witnesses through whom the message of Light and Life shall flow to all men.

During the persecutions in England under Queen Mary in the sixteenth century, Bishops Hugh Latimer and Nicholas Ridley were being burned at the stake, martyrs for Christ. Ridley cried, "Master Latimer, it is more than I can bear. Shall I not recant?" "Be of good comfort, Master Ridley," cried Latimer, "and play the man. We shall this day light such a candle by God's grace, in England, as I trust shall never be put out."

Because John the Baptist was faithful, because Christians through the centuries were faithful, we have opportunity today to be faithful as well. In the name of everything that is right and holy we must answer the question, "Can I do less?"

8. False Lights

"He was not that Light, but was sent to bear witness of that Light" (John 1:8).

THE APOSTLE JOHN reminds us that John the Baptist, great as he was, was not the true Light, and that men must not put their faith in him lest they be disappointed. He seems to be saying "Don't let the fact that I have introduced a man to give witness to the truth of the Light confuse you. Don't give too much attention to the man." John, the beloved apostle, was warning us of a very real and important danger. How many young Christians have fallen because of the actions of someone in whom they had trusted? How important that we do not put too much faith in the one who is the witness to the Light. We must trust, rather, in Him who is the Light.

The World Congress on Youth Evangelism in Beirut, Lebanon, had as its theme, "The Changeless Christ for a Changing World." What a pity that many of the speakers had much more to say about the changing world than they did about the changeless Christ. We do well when we keep our eyes on Him.

There are two things in life which primarily disappoint us: circumstances and people. Adam must surely have been disappointed when his wife sinned and his son killed his brother. I think of Noah's disappointment when not one person believed his message outside of his own family, or Joseph's disappointment in Egypt when his brothers had sold him into slavery. Or Moses, when he returned from the Mount of the Commandments to find the people in idolatry. Or Paul, when he writes, "Demas hath forsaken me, having loved this present world" (2 Tim. 4:10). And surely our Lord had more reason to be disappointed than anyone else who ever lived. Yet a strong and confident faith in His heavenly Father saved Him from disappointment because He knew all men.

John's introduction of a human personality into his prologue is not intended to give too much emphasis to John the Baptist. Stop a minute, he seems to warn. Don't be confused. This man was a witness, not a Light. Jesus was the true Light, John was only the witness who came to tell us about the Light.

To save us from disappointment, it is imperative that we have a correct view of God and a correct view of His Word and revelation. Too many of us view the circumstances of life with far too great importance, ending in our own frustration. There have been many false lights. Gautama Buddha came six hundred years before the birth of Christ and Mohammed came about the same number after Christ. Both declared themselves sent from God. But those who hope to find everlasting life from mere men such as they will find only disappointment.

The subapostolic times produced at least fifty pseudepigraphal writings containing about seven or eight gospels in addition to the four canonical Gospels. Those who hope to find eternal life in these writings are bound to

be disappointed. Joseph Smith came, and Joseph Ruth-
erford and Charles Russell, and Mary Baker Eddy, with
their failure to point men adequately to the true Light.
Their writings are bound to disappoint.

Modern Zionism teaches that Israel herself is the Messiah, that the Messiah is not a person but a nation. What
a pity! Jesus is the true Light. The writer to the Hebrews
declares that Jesus is the express image of God (Heb.
1:3). The word *express* means exact, complete. Jesus is
the full, complete, exact, precise image of God. In Him
dwells all the fullness of the Godhead bodily (Col. 2:9).
He is the Alpha and Omega—the All in all.

If you put too much faith in men, you are bound to be
disappointed. Turn your eyes upon Jesus. Keep your
faith in Him. He is the true Light and will not disappoint you.

The Apostle John warns that men must be guided,
enlightened by true light and not false. What are the
tests by which one can determine that the light upon his
way is true light and not false? For one thing, the false
light emphasizes the present. It takes the short look. It is
only concerned with now. There is something about
Satan and his false light that is always in a hurry. He will
always sacrifice the peace and ultimate good of tomorrow
for a taste of the forbidden fruit today. The immediate
appeasement of the flesh forgets the ultimate end of life.

Harry Emerson Fosdick said there is a price to be paid
either way in life. One can have the diamond now and
the dust later, or the dust now and diamonds later. A
false light always emphasizes the immediate. A little
cheating here and there on a business deal may satisfy
the hunger for immediate success, but a true light points
to the long look. Esau sold his birthright for the sake

of the immediate appeasement of his hunger. Peter submitted to the howling crowd and lost his fellowship with Christ. Judas took the short look and betrayed the Master for thirty pieces of silver. Not to mention Samson, David, and a thousand others who lived a life of regret from a decision that involved a short look.

Second, a false light illuminates everything except the true light. The modern church is cumbered with a hundred theologies and philosophies that emphasize everything from the Holy Spirit to social reform, from tongues and ecstatic experience to prophecies of the future. It is even possible to practice bibliolatry, the worship of the Bible, so that Bible study becomes an end in itself and men become hearers of the Word more than doers. The touchstone of every doctrine, of every theology, of every question is "What place does it give to Jesus Christ?"

Third, a true light illuminates the hopelessness of man's self-righteousness. A true light does not testify "What a wonderful change in my life has been wrought, Since *catechism* came into my heart," or "Since *baptism* came into my heart." The true testimony is, rather, "Since Jesus came into my heart." A false light exalts the works of the flesh, but the true Light illuminates the soul and exposes the inadequacies of the flesh. We are filled with the light of His grace.

Caesar Clark tells the story of an eight-year-old boy who decided that his mother asked too much of him and decided to charge her for his services. One morning at the breakfast table he quietly slipped a note beneath her plate which read, "Cleaning my room 7 days—10¢ per day—Charge—70¢." His mother gladly paid the bill, only to find another one a few days later: "Picking up toys—40¢. Mowing the yard—$1.30." One day the boy overslept and came belatedly to the breakfast table to find a note from his mother. Eagerly he opened it and began to read from the top:

"For going down into the valley of the shadow of death to bring you into the world—No Charge.

"For staying up with you all night when you were at the point of death and praying to God through the midnight hours until the fever broke—No Charge.

"For cooking your meals three times a day for seven days a week for eight years—No Charge!"

No Charge!

Centuries ago God looked down into the world and saw the bankrupt human race lost in the darkness of sin. Because He loved the world, He sent the Light of the world, the true Light, with a message from heaven. "For dying on an old rugged cross when they spat in my face and rejected and cursed me, for hanging naked on a tree for your sins—No Charge.

"For going down into the grave and grappling with the powers of sin, death, hell and the grave for three days, and coming forth victorious—No Charge.

"For preparing a place for you in heaven and coming again for you to receive you unto myself that where I am, there you may be also—No Charge. No Charge!"

The world is overrun with false lights shining this way and that, with false theologies and false religions which have one thing in common—the exaltation of the deeds of the flesh. But they are false lights. Jesus paid it *all* on the cross, and writes across our debt, "No Charge." Salvation is by His grace. He and He alone is the true Light that lighteth every man who cometh into the world.

9. Light to Every Man

"That was the true Light, which lighteth every man that cometh into the world" (John 1:9).

IN THESE WORDS John uses a common but very significant word—*every*. He tells us the good news that the true Light lights *every* man that comes into the world.

Few questions have intrigued us more than the matter of the destiny of those who have never heard the gospel. John speaks frankly to the point that every man has received light for which he is responsible, for Jesus Christ faithfully lights every man that comes into the world. There is much that we do not know about the ways of God with men. But consider five aspects of this important matter that we do know:

1. We know that if there is a God, the burden of any revealing of Himself rests with Him and not with us. God has more than adequately fulfilled that responsibility. John records that He has given us life, light to know how to use the life, a witness to know about the light, and grace to live the life. This is Christianity's distinctive— God seeking man; God reaching from heaven to say, "I love you. I have given you the gift of life, and the reason is love."

People often say, "If there is a God why doesn't He do something supernatural to reveal Himself to man?" But God has done something fantastic. He has taken the initiative. Because He so loved the world, He gave His only begotten Son to live and die as a man—and as if that wasn't enough, He brought again our Lord Jesus from the dead!

In His parable of the rich man and Lazarus, Jesus has Abraham tell the rich man, who pleaded in Hades for a special revelation to his brothers by a miraculous resurrection, "They have Moses and the prophets; . . . if they hear not [them], neither will they be persuaded, though one rose from the dead" (Luke 16:29, 31).

God revealed Himself in the dark hour of human need and He continues to reveal Himself to all who seek Him. Seneca said that man in his natural condition is keenly aware of his helplessness in necessary things. But the Bible shows us that he must always take the first step of faith and respond to the revelation of God before he can know Him fully.

2. We know that if there is a God, He is fair and just. Listen to the message of Scripture. Leviticus says that the judgments of God require us to use just weights and measures (Lev. 19:36). In Deuteronomy, God requires of His people just and righteous judgment in court cases (Deut. 16:18–20)—a theme which the Hebrew prophets used again and again (Amos 5:15, 24; Hos. 12:6; Isa. 56:1). Ezekiel echoes the call of Leviticus for just weights and balances (Ezek. 45:9–10). Nehemiah says the Lord is just (Neh. 9:33). Abraham said of God, "Shall not the Judge of all the earth do right?" (Gen. 18:25). Revelation records the song sung in heaven: "Just and true are thy ways, thou King of saints" (Rev. 15:3).

God does not send babies and people with limited intellectual capacity or the mentally defective (idiots, imbeciles and morons) to hell. God is a just God. Paul makes it clear that no man will be able to say that God was unjust (Rom. 2:1–11).

3. We know that universally men sense their need of a relationship with a higher power. To whatever group or tribe civilization has gone, no matter how primitive, it has found men seeking to appease deity for their sins, whether they considered deity invisible or resident in animals or trees or other objects. Long before God established the Levitical system, men were offering burnt sacrifices in appeasement to their gods. Somehow the misty smoke must have seemed to be a link between the visible and the invisible, as they sent their sacrifice wafting into the heavens where lived the powers that were greater than they. As man cries out to God, he scans the skies, sensing, feeling, believing that somehow, somewhere, someone is out there.

4. God has revealed Himself through many means and varied ways to all men. This is what the writer to the Hebrews declares: "God, who at sundry times and in divers manners spake in time past unto the fathers by the prophets, hath in these last days spoken unto us by his Son" (Heb. 1:1–2). "The wrath of God is revealed from heaven against all ungodliness and unrighteousness," says the Apostle Paul (Rom. 1:18).

Not only has God revealed Himself to all men through His Son, but He has made all men aware of their need and intends to judge all men for their unrighteousness. Paul declares in the first chapter of Romans that the invisible things of God "from the creation of the world are clearly seen, being understood by the things that are made, even his eternal power and Godhead" (Rom. 1:20). The heavens declare the glory of God (Ps. 19:1), and the trees and the rivers and the mountains and the nations declare the reality of God, but they only declare the reality of God in His *power.* It therefore becomes the responsibility of the Christian witness to declare the reality of God in His *love,* for nature does not speak of the love of God, merely His reality and the power.

God has spoken to man in nature, in the heavens, in his conscience, in a mother's smile, in a baby's face, in the gentle touch of a father. He has revealed Himself in many ways to all men. God has made all men aware. He has illuminated the hearts of men. The Light has shined into the heart of every man who has come into the world. It then becomes the responsibility of the witness to give testimony to the love of God.

5. It is, therefore, true that the ultimate revelation of God's love is committed to people who have experienced that love. There are those who suggest that man can never know he is lost and doomed until he has heard the message of God and rejected it. But if this were the case, we would run the risk of doing more harm than good by taking the gospel to men. For if they were better off never having heard, our Lord would have never commanded us to go into all the world and preach the gospel to every creature.

This is precisely what our faith is all about. It is what missions and evangelism are all about. It is said that 175,000 people per day are born into the world, and that the great majority will die never having heard the name of Christ. Eight million a year in India alone die never having heard the name of Jesus.

The burden of missions, the responsibility of bearing

witness to the Light, is ours. The missionary ramifications of John 1:9 are never ending. We have been entrusted with the true Light that lights every man that comes into the world. The Light is there. The knowledge and direction are there. The awareness of need is there. But it is only as Christians witness that the Light can be intelligently comprehended in the person of Jesus Christ. May God help us to cooperate with Him in the task of world evangelism—the challenge of bearing witness to the Light.

10. The Light in the World

"He was in the world, and the world was made by him, and the world knew him not" (John 1:10).

JESUS CAME to His own people as their Messiah and to the world-at-large as its Creator. In verse 10 of the prologue John states three simple truths about Christ's coming. The first is that "He was in the world."

That Jesus was in the world is the undisputed and indisputable fact of history. As Dr. James Allan Francis, pastor of the First Baptist Church of Los Angeles for many years, put it so well in his sermon "One Solitary Life":

Here is a man who was born in an obscure village, the Child of a peasant woman. He worked in a carpenter shop until He was thirty, and then for three years He was an itinerant preacher.

He never wrote a book. He never held an office. He never owned a home. He never had a family. He never went to college. He never put his foot inside a big city. He never traveled two hundred miles from the place where He was born.

He never did one of the things that usually accompany greatness. He had no credentials but Himself. He had

nothing to do with this world except the naked power of
His Divine manhood.

While still a young man, the tide of popular opinion
turned against Him. He was turned over to His enemies.
He went through the mockery of a trial. He was nailed
to a Cross between two thieves. His executioners gambled
for the only piece of property He had on earth while He
was dying—and that was His Coat.

When He was dead He was taken down and laid in a
borrowed grave through the pity of a friend. Such was His
human life—He rises from the dead.

Nineteen wide centuries have come and gone and today
He is the Centerpiece of the human race and the Leader
of the column of progress.

I am within the mark when I say that all the armies that
ever marched, and all the navies that ever were built, and
all the parliaments that ever sat, and all the kings that
ever reigned, put together, have not affected the life of
man upon this earth as powerfully as that One Solitary
Life.

We can add that though He was not primarily a so-
ciologist, He has done more good for society than all the
sociologists combined. Though not primarily a psycholo-
gist, He is the great Creator of human personality and
the solution to its needs. Though He never sang a song,
more songs have been sung of Him than all the themes
of the world combined. Though He never wrote a book,
more books have been written about Him than can ever
be numbered. Calendars are dated from His birth. Dying saints have found hope and strength as they hold fast
by faith to Him.

The reality of Jesus Christ, of the historical Christ, is
one of the best documented facts of history. The test

of the eyewitness, the test of endurance, the test of believability—all of those means by which historians give weight to the validity of historical facts, when applied to Jesus Christ, make Him the most real, profound, and positive fact of recorded history. Where his influence has gone, hospitals have been built and orphanages established. Alfred Edersheim, one of the great Jewish historians of all time, wrote a book entitled *The Life and Times of Jesus the Messiah* in which he set out to document the historical fact of Christ scientifically and intellectually. Years later, at the conclusion of his life and of his great work, Mr. Edersheim said, "If Jesus Christ did not live and He was not the Son of God and He is not the Messiah, then there never has been a Messiah and there never will be!" To deny that Jesus came into the world, to deny the historical fact of Christ in the face of the overwhelming evidence of Scripture and history is to approach the precipice of absurdity.

The second truth John gives us in this verse is that the world was made by Jesus Christ. The word *world, kosmos* in the Greek, does not simply mean mankind, but includes the whole of creation—the heavens, the stars, the galaxies, the planets, the earth . . . all of it. Jesus came to the innkeeper and the innkeeper had no place for Him. He was the Creator of the sheep who moved aside that He might have a place for His birth.

When Jesus came to the earth, the earth knew Him not. The earth had made no provision for her Creator. Though He had created the birds and their nests, there was found no home for the Savior. Born in a borrowed stable, He took a borrowed name from His mother's husband that He might have a legal name for legal purposes. When He would feed the multitude, He borrowed the loaves and fishes from a small boy. He rode into Jerusalem on the back of a borrowed donkey. He was tried in a borrowed robe and buried in a borrowed tomb! Only His cross was His own. The only earthly possession that He ever had outside of His own clothes was His cross. He was in the world and the world was made by Him.

The third fact given in this verse is that the world knew Him not. What a pity that men chose—and still choose—not to know Him. The word *knew* is from the Greek verb *ginōskō,* which is the root of our English words *knowledge, know.* When we place the syllable *a* in front of that, it totally reverses it. It makes it void. It makes something of nothing. From *ginōskō* comes *gnostic,* meaning "one who knows." But, when we add the prefix *a-* to it, we create the word *agnostic,* which means "not to know." So, when a man says that "I do not know him," he is saying, "I am ignorant." Ignorant men ought not to be followed. Jesus said, "I am come that they might have life," and "He that believeth on me hath everlasting life" (John 10:10; 6:47). But the world would not have His life. The world would not know or believe in Him. They refused the Light. They rejected their Creator.

Throughout history mankind has sought to know God. Tolstoy said that to know God is hard. Hegel said that we must know God intellectually. Edward Gibbon, English historian, said that we can never really know God. But Hume, the English philosopher, said that we can only know God through faith. Sir Isaac Newton said that we know Him through order in His universe.

But most men choose not to know Him. In so doing, they turn the gladdest fact in history, the coming of the Light of the world, into the awfulness of blackest night for themselves. They do not know Him, for they will not to know Him, their understanding being darkened by the blindness of sin. They do not understand that God had condescended to become a man. They will not understand that life comes by death, and he that would find his life must lose it for Jesus' sake. They will not believe the irrevocable principle upon which all the biblical doctrine of the remission of sin is based—the death of the innocent for the guilty. They do not and will not believe because they are blind—blinded by Satan, the god of this world (2 Cor. 4:4). The Apostle Paul says that because of their blindness, God gave them up to uncleanness. God gave them up to vile affections because they would not retain God in their knowledge (Rom. 1:18–32). Paul does not say that men could not retain God in their knowledge; he says that "they did not like to"—they *would* not (Rom. 1:28).

Jesus prayed over Jerusalem, "O Jerusalem, Jerusalem, thou that killest the prophets, and stonest them which are sent unto thee, how often would I have gathered thy children together, even as a hen gathereth her chickens under her wings, and ye would not!" (Matt. 23:37). It was not that they could not, but that they would not.

The world's rejection of her Creator, her Savior, is willful and determined. How much is lost when men will not so relate themselves to the Savior, when they *will* not come unto Him that they might have life eternal.

11. The Messiah

"He came unto his own, and his own received him not"
(John 1:11).

GOD ALWAYS does things on time. God had promised
Abraham and Sarah a son. Yet after scores of years, no
son had been born. Finally, in the fullness of time, when
things were ready, God sent a child by miraculous birth.
For four hundred years Israel had cried for deliverance
from Egyptian bondage. When all things were ready, God
answered, He sent Moses to bring the people out of
Egypt into the promised land.

Just so, the Bible had prophesied that the Messiah was
to come as a root out of dry ground (Isa. 53:2). That is,
when things were at a low spiritual ebb, in an unlikely
time, the Messiah would be born—born in the fullness
of time. At last, all things were right and "he came unto
his own." The expression "his own" in the Greek is
neuter plural, which means simply, He came to His own
things. That is, He came not merely to His own people,
but to His own city, His own lifestyle, His own land, as
well as His own people.

But though they were His own people and country,
His own received Him not. How could the Jews reject

their Savior? There are at least five reasons, and they are the same basic reasons that men reject the Christ today.

1. The Jews rejected Jesus because their eyes were blinded to scriptural truth. Too often we seek to know God's will apart from the Scripture. We seek for feeling and circumstance, but God sends His word.

The Old Testament was very clear about the Messiah's coming. Yet with minds filled with preconceptions and hearts blinded by sin, the Jews searched the Scriptures for references to the Messiah, but they did not find or recognize Jesus Christ. Through the centuries they had read the prophets—Isaiah, Zechariah, Daniel, Malachi—all of them had testified of Him. Jesus said, "Search the scriptures; for . . . they are they which testify of me" (John 5:39).

The Jews had ears to hear but they would not hear. They had eyes to see, yet they would not or could not see (Matt. 13:13). The fifty-third chapter of Isaiah looks with prophetic insight toward the Messiah's rejection and asks, "Who hath believed our report?" Then the chapter goes on to describe the suffering Christ. "He shall grow up before him as a tender plant." Jesus Christ was the most tender person who ever lived. He came "as a root out of a dry ground," at an unlikely time in history.

"He hath no form nor comeliness; and when we shall see him, there is no beauty that we should desire him. He is . . . a man of sorrows, and acquainted with grief: . . . and we esteemed him not" (Isa. 53:2–3). Literally, His appearance as He became sin for us was so ghastly, so distorted that we could not look upon Him. "He is despised and rejected of men . . . and we hid as it were our faces from him . . . he was wounded for our transgressions" (vv.

3, 5). The chapter goes on to tell of the stripes and
bruises Jesus Christ received for us, describing His crucifixion and death for our sins. "And he made his grave
with the wicked, and with the rich in his death" (v. 9).
This was fulfilled when, on Calvary, Jesus was crucified
between two sinful men and then was buried in the
grave of a rich man—the borrowed tomb of wealthy
Joseph of Arimathaea. "Therefore," says God, "will I
divide him a portion with the great." Here He is in resur-
rected power. "And he shall divide the spoil with the
strong; because he hath poured out his soul unto death:
and he was numbered with the transgressors; and he bare
the sin of many and made intercession for the transgressors" (v. 12).

It is difficult for me to see how this, one of the clearest
of Messianic passages, could be read with an open mind
and a spiritually enlightened heart by the Jews and not
apply it to the Christ. But the Jews applied it to the
nation of Israel. Their eyes were blinded and they could
not and would not see.

2. The Jews rejected Jesus because of their pride.
They had a fierce pride in their heritage. How many
times did they cry to Jesus, "What need have we of thee?"
"We have Abraham to our father," was their attitude.
"We be Abraham's seed" (Matt. 3:9; John 8:33). But
Jesus told them, "Ye are of your father the devil" (John
8:44).

They were proud of being Abraham's children after
the flesh. Jesus called them proselyters and warned that
they compassed sea and land to make a single convert, but
made him instead twicefold a child of hell (Matt. 23:15).
They were proud of their proselyting, proud of their
position, proud of their heritage. They loved the promi-

nent places in the synagogues. They loved to pray standing in the streets. They loved to display their phylacteries
(Matt. 6:5; 23:5–7). And they paid dearly to hold positions of great prominence. They were not about to give
them up in humility to some carpenter's son. They lived
for the public. They loved to lead the parade, to be seen
of men. But Jesus came and said, "The last shall be
first" (Matt. 20:16), and, "Whosoever will save his life
shall lose it" (Luke 9:24). "For whosoever exalteth himself shall be abased; and he that humbleth himself shall
be exalted" (Luke 14:11). But the teaching ran cross-
grain to their pride.

Worst of all, the Jews were proud of themselves. When
they brought to Jesus a woman taken in adultery, Jesus
said to them, "He that is without sin among you, let him
first cast a stone at her." One by one the woman's accusers
left His presence. They could not face Him—but they
would not accept Him (John 8:1–11).

3. The Jews rejected Jesus because they were looking
for an earthly kingdom. For centuries they had been
suppressed under the harsh Roman Empire. They ex-
pected that the Messiah would come with great earthly
power and overthrow their physical enemies, making the
Jewish nation free and autonomous. More than anything,
they longed for physical deliverance and power.

Even Jesus' disciples had this idea. Just before Jesus'
ascension, they asked Him, "Lord, wilt thou at this time
restore again the kingdom to Israel?" Jesus had tried to
tell them that His kingdom was an inner kingdom of
love and truth in the heart, but he told them now, "It is
not for you to know the times or the seasons, which the
Father hath put in his own power" (Acts 1:6–7). It was
not for them to know when the King would come in

glory or when His earthly kingdom would begin. Your job, he told them, is to go "into all the world, and preach the gospel to every creature" (Mark 16:15). For now the kingdom of God is within you (Luke 17:21). But for the proud Jews, Caesar, as bad as he was, was to be preferred above Christ because he was an earthly king with earthly power. They hated Caesar, but still they acclaimed, "We have no king but Caesar," because in their minds, Jesus was no king at all. "Away with him," they shouted, "away with him, crucify him" (John 19:14–15).

The Jews rejected Jesus because they misunderstood the nature of the kingdom. They looked for an immediate solution to their earthly problems. Just so, men misinterpret the kingdom today. For, if the kingdom of Christ were only an immediate solution to all physical problems, men would become Christians for the wrong reasons.

4. The Jews rejected Jesus because it would cost them their jobs to follow Him. The Apostle John records their attitude in chapter 11, verses 46 to 48. "But some of them went their ways to the Pharisees, and told them what things Jesus had done. Then gathered the chief priests and the Pharisees a council, and said, What do we? for this man doeth many miracles. If we let him thus alone, all men will believe on him: and the Romans shall come and take away both our place and nation." If we do not do something, they were saying, all the common people will respond to Jesus and we will lose our status, our positions, our jobs. There is a price to be paid for following Jesus, and it was one they were not willing to pay.

In Judaism, positions of honor in the synagogues could be purchased for money. Men of prestigious and wealthy families had paid dearly to purchase these positions for their own use. To be a member of the Sanhedrin, the governing council, cost money, and to follow Jesus would have meant the loss of position and financial power. How familiar it sounds today. If we follow Christ, we may lose our place, we may lose our position. "Away with him, crucify him." Hang onto the job; hang onto the almighty dollar. Possession at any cost—that is the name of the game.

5. They rejected Jesus simply because they waited too long. Jesus warned their cities of impending doom and told them that if the mighty works that had been done in them had been done in Sodom, or Tyre and Sidon, those cities would have repented and been intact to this very day (Matt. 11:20–24). At another time he warned the Jews of the unpardonable sin, when men's hearts are so hardened by constant rejection of the Holy Spirit's call that they can no longer will the good, they can bring forth no good thing (Matt. 12:31–32). They have lost the power to believe, the capability of faith.

It is said that shortly before going to his death, Hermann Göring, executioner of six million Jews, was visited by his sister, who asked to speak with him. When asked the nature of her visit, she said that she had become a Christian and wanted to tell her brother about Christ and ask him to repent of his sins and trust the Savior. Göring slammed the door on her with an oath and said, "No, I settled that issue a long time ago!" In less than two hours, Göring had taken his own life, before justice could be executed on him. Each of us must face the issue of Christ and the eternal question of the ages, "What will you do with Christ, the Light of the world, Jesus of Nazareth?"

12. The Gift of God

"But as many as received him, to them gave he power to become the sons of God, even to them that believe on his name" (John 1:12).

THE TWELFTH verse of John's prologue is perhaps the most comprehensive salvation verse in John's Gospel. Let us note five great truths it contains.

First of all, it speaks of the intervention of God. Verse 10 speaks of the world's rejection of Christ, verse 11, of His rejection by the Jews. But God does not give up. He will not leave man to his own designs. In *love,* God intervened in human affairs. Though the world rejected Jesus Christ and His people rejected Him, to as many as did receive Him He gave the power—authority—to become the children of God.

In the midst of this negative reaction, John gives us the dynamic assertion of the positive. In the midst of death, the introduction of the Light. In the midst of despair, a word of hope. Though many rejected, some did receive! Here is the assurance that God is still on the throne. No negative antagonism is too great for Him. He will still write the last chapter of history. All things are still working and will work together for good for those who love the Lord. The Devil is not going to write the last chapter of history.

John not only speaks of divine intervention, he speaks also of divine inclusiveness. There were *many* who received Jesus Christ. I like that word *many,* because it indicates a great amount of people. In his apocalyptic vision, the writer of Revelation saw the rebelling Satan draw a third of the angels of heaven after him, and all were cast out of heaven (Rev. 12:3–4; 9–10). But two-thirds of the angels did not follow Satan. God always has His own. Though the Jews as a nation rejected Jesus as their Messiah, there still have always been the great Jewish believers—the Peters, Jameses, Johns, and Pauls, the Edersheims, the Appelmans. As *many* as received Him.

It is said that up until modern times, as many as two-thirds of the babies born into this world died before the age of five due to the worldwide prevalence of killing diseases. These little ones have gone to heaven. Could it be that there will be more souls in heaven than in hell after all? Exodus records the reaction of Pharaoh to the people of God, the children of Israel—"the people are many" (Exod. 5:5). Numbers records the reaction of the Moabites to the Israelites—they were distressed because they were many; "they cover the face of the earth; . . . they are too mighty" (Num. 22:3–6). Isaiah speaks of many people saying, "Come . . . and let us go up to the . . . house of . . . God" (Isa. 2:3). Jesus says, "Go out into the highways and hedges, and compel them to come in, that my house may be filled" (Luke 14:23). The writer of Revelation describes the saints in heaven as "a great multitude, which no man could number" (Rev. 7:9). All of this is hinted at in John's positive word that many would and did receive Jesus.

Third, there is here a divine invitation. It is the invitation to receive Jesus Christ. It is important to remember the word *him* in the phrase "as many as received him." The marvel and mystery of the Christian gospel is that it is centered in a person, Jesus Christ. John does not say, "As many as receive baptism," or "As many as receive the church," or "As many as receive his teachings or precepts." It is to "as many as received him" that God gave the authority to be His children. Baptism is important. It is a command of Christ to follow Him therein upon our conversion. But baptism is to be received *following* salvation. The church is ordained and established by Christ. He is coming again for His church, and glory and honor are in His church. But it is not to as many as received the church that the power was given to become the sons of God. It is as many as received *Him*.

No man ever taught as Jesus taught. Listen again: "Blessed are the poor in spirit: for theirs is the kingdom of heaven. Blessed are they that mourn: for they shall be comforted. Blessed are the meek: for they shall inherit the earth. Blessed are they which do hunger and thirst after righteousness: for they shall be filled. Blessed are the merciful: for they shall obtain mercy. Blessed are the pure in heart: for they shall see God. Blessed are the peacemakers: for they shall be called the children of God. Blessed are they which are persecuted for righteousness' sake: for theirs is the kingdom of heaven" (Matt. 5:3–10). Never a man taught like this.

But salvation is not found simply in His beautiful teachings. If I place a dollar bill inside a book and offer it to you, you must accept the book to receive the dollar because the dollar is in the book. Salvation is in Jesus Christ. You cannot receive salvation unless you receive

Christ. He does not simply offer salvation. It is not an attribute of His. It is in Him. He personally must be experienced. He personally must be received.

Fourth, there is suggested here a divine impartation. "As many as received him, to them gave he power to become the sons of God." The word *power* is the Greek word *exousia,* which is a multifaceted word. For one thing, it includes the power to choose. Intellectually we may think we know how we would like to choose, but only as Christ is in us and we in Him do we have the power to make right choices. Paul says Christ works in us both to will and to do His good pleasure (Phil. 2:13). To have the power to choose to do right is one thing. To have the power to do the right thing is quite another, but that power is given us as well, because we have become God's children.

To receive Him is also to have the power of authority. Jesus said, "All power [*exousia,* authority] is given unto me in heaven and in earth," and "Whatsoever ye shall bind on earth shall be bound in heaven: and whatsoever ye shall loose on earth shall be loosed in heaven" (Matt. 28:18; 18:18). He gives us divine authority when He gives us heavenly power.

This power is ours when we believe on His name. John does not say *"in* his name" (the Greek says "into his name"), for there is far more entailed than a simple adherence to the reality of the historical Christ. No more than a drowning man can be saved by believing intellectually that a life raft would save him can we be saved by believing that the historical Christ could save. The man must believe *on* the raft, must entrust himself to it. Just so must we entrust ourselves to Jesus Christ.

We have seen that the grand twelfth verse of John's

prologue contains a divine intervention of God who would not give up on His beloved creation, a divine inclusiveness to as *many* as would receive, and a divine invitation to receive Jesus Christ, coupled with a divine impartation—the giving of His power. But last, it contains a divine inheritance—the power to become the sons of God.

A son has a right to everything that is his father's. He has his father's image, his father's assets, his father's name, his father's home, his father's personality, and his father's inheritance. The two are by relationship one. As believers we never need to say that we are poor. While we might not own a nickel of this world's goods, we are children of God and brothers of Jesus Christ and thereby rich men. Jesus Christ, "though he was rich, yet for your sakes he became poor, that ye through his poverty might be rich" (2 Cor. 8:9).

When the prodigal son returned home, the father gave him a new robe for his back, new shoes for his feet, and a new ring for his finger. Everything that belonged to the father belonged to the son.

Do you personally know Jesus Christ? Can you say with confidence, "I have received Christ in person and He is mine and I am His"? To know Christ is to have life everlasting. To know Him is to possess the characteristics of God, because in His Son dwells all the fullness of the Godhead bodily (Col. 2:9). That same fullness, that same power, those same possessions, can be yours in Jesus Christ.

13. Born of God

"Which were born, not of blood, nor of the will of the flesh, nor of the will of man, but of God" (John 1:13).

AT THE THIRTEENTH verse of his prologue, John moves from the area of the philosophical to the realm of the experiential. We have been given the glad news that though some reject the Word, those that did receive Him were given power to become the sons of God.

The sons of God—what a staggering concept that is! The idea that one's relationship with God could be that of a father and son was a generally new one for the Jews, though it was hinted at by some of the Old Testament writers (e.g., Ps. 103:13; Isa. 63:16; Jer. 31:9). The idea of becoming a son of God must have filled their minds with wonder unspeakable.

We, too, should be filled with awe at this great privilege. John tells us clearly the exclusive means by which we may, indeed, become God's own children. In this one verse he clears the air of all confusion and speculation, and cuts the ground from beneath every fallacy regarding an important truth—the method of spiritual birth and relationship.

First, to become a child of God does not mean to be

born of blood. It is a spiritual experience, not a physical birth. A spiritual inheritance is not passed on through normal physical means, that is, through blood descent. Mothers and fathers do not pass on spiritual propensities to their children through their genes. The expression John uses is plural, literally, "of bloods." The union of the parents, the life produced by the joining of two organisms, the union of the mother's and father's bloods, cannot produce spiritual life.

As suggested earlier, the Jews were particularly proud of their heritage, and reminded Jesus that they were Abraham's seed, that royal blood ran in their veins. Jesus cut them to the quick when He reminded them that they were in fact of their father the devil, because physical blood did not transmit spiritual righteousness (John 8:31–59). The Spanish aristocrats coined the phrase "blue blood" because they believed that a different kind of blood flowed through their veins that was bluer than ordinary blood. The term has come to stand for supposed superiority because of birth—as the blue blood of royalty or nobility. John warns that too much emphasis must not be given to the heritage of physical bloods. Paul stated, "I know that in me (that is, in my flesh,) dwelleth no good thing" (Rom. 7:18).

Nothing is more beautiful than a mother and father filled with pride at the birth of a son or daughter. But we must remind ourselves that within that beautiful baby there is the potential to do every wrong and to commit every sin in the category of hell apart from God's saving grace. That is a hard concept for us to accept. Many believe that they are Christians because they were born into a Christian home or have been educated in

Christian universities or are the sons of Christian parents. But John makes it very clear that they may become children of God only by receiving Jesus Christ.

Jesus explained to Nicodemus the necessity for the new birth. To be living at all, one must have been born of the womb, born of the water birth, the physical human birth through which human bloodlines flow. But to enter the kingdom of God, a person must be born again, he must experience the second birth, the spiritual birth from above (John 3:1-8). There must be a change of heart before children of Satan may become children of God.

Second, John states that we may become children of God, but not by the will of the flesh. That is to say, spiritual birth is not the effort of mere human goodness. Jesus was born into a world characterized by human religious effort. Rules governed every action of man. The students of the law had devised rules to cover every conceivable kind of situation. The law allowed a person to travel no more than two hundred steps on the Sabbath, since a longer journey would be working on the Sabbath. A man finding himself in the middle of the street on his two-hundredth step technically should stand there with one foot raised in the air until the Sabbath was over. Otherwise he would be sinning by breaking the law. But then the question should be asked, "When is the Sabbath over?" Is it when the sun goes down? When is the sun down? When the bottom of it sinks beneath the horizon? When it is half down? All the way down? Or, is it when its last golden rays have ceased to shine? There were more than 600 such rules which a good Jew should keep. Entirely too much emphasis was given to the action and effort of men and too little to the divine operation of the Spirit creating new life through new birth in the human heart.

Time and again Jesus scores the Pharisees with being hypocrites, their supposed righteousness, in Isaiah's terms, no better than filthy rags (Isa. 64:6). Their good works, apart from grace, were merely a pile of filthy embalming rags taken from a decaying and rotting corpse. "Whited sepulchres" he called them (Matt. 23:27; cf. 23:1–36).

Perhaps no doctrine should be more clearly stated than that true spiritual life must be evidenced by good works. But it must be equally stated that no work, no effort of man's will, can produce even the slightest contribution to the finished work of Christ. Nothing—no baptism, no church ordinance, no effort of prayer or Bible reading, no work however good—nothing that is produced by mere human effort can contribute one whit to Christ's grace. It will not get you born into God's kingdom and family. "For by grace are ye saved through faith; and that not of yourselves"—not by the will of man—"it is the gift of God" (Eph. 2:8).

Third, John states that it is not by the will of man that we are born into heavenly relationship with God. Through history men have attempted to impart salvation through pronouncement. John says it is not the mere sprinkling of a few rose water words in some ordinance that makes you a child of God. It is not the "well done" of a preacher or priest. In the fourth century the Emperor Constantine pronounced the world Christian, but in reality it was not. More than the will of one man is required for the world to become Christian, for salvation must be a personal experience. No church can pronounce you Christian because you have joined its membership or been baptized. No mother and father can pronounce you Christian because they have had you sprinkled. It is not by the will of man.

It is possible for erroneous theology to create situations in which one man can pronounce or confer salvation upon another man—can literally become his God, the agent of salvation. Follow that theory to its ultimate conclusion. Suppose you and I are marooned on an island, an island from which we will never depart alive, and you come to me wishing to be saved. Then you ask me to baptize you in order to procure your salvation and I refuse to do so. I become God. I possess within my will the power to send you to heaven or to send you to hell. Your spiritual relationship to God is at the mercy of a man. In His last moments on the cross, Jesus cried, "It is finished," that is, that salvation's plan was finished. There is, therefore, nothing that man can do to add to or take therefrom.

May the Lord help us as Christians, as churches, as pastors to reaffirm our commitment to the declaration of this imperative message, that men might be related to God, not by blood, not by the will of the flesh, nor by the will of man, but by being born of the Spirit of God.

> Blessed assurance, Jesus is mine,
> Oh, what a foretaste of glory divine.
> Heir of salvation, purchase of God,
> Born of His Spirit, washed in His blood.
> —FANNY J. CROSBY

14. The Word Made Flesh

"And the Word was made flesh, and dwelt among us, (and we beheld his glory, the glory as of the only begotten of the Father,) full of grace and truth" (John 1:14).

THE FOURTEENTH verse of John's prologue is an amplification of the first verse. Having introduced the Word, Jesus Christ, as the Creator of the world, eternal God, eternal Lord, John introduces Him in the form of flesh, in the form of a man, as the Word made flesh. It was that men might understand this truth that the entire book was written. The Word made flesh, God tabernacling in human form, is the prologue's story. It is the Christmas story. It is the gospel story. Jesus Christ laid aside His regal robes of royalty and stepped to the earth through the womb of the Virgin. The very Creator came to be the Savior, humbling Himself in the fashion of a man, becoming obedient unto the death of a cross, divesting Himself of His glory as God to take part in everything that was ours as humans.

Once Charlemagne was given a drink from the blood-stained helmet of one of his dying soldiers in the sweltering desert. The great general refused to drink until all of his soldiers had first drunk. When they finished, it is said that there was none left for him. But no earthly act of human condescension ever approached that of our Lord Jesus when He, the eternal Word, became flesh. It is more staggering than if an archangel had become a bumble bee, or a king become a pauper.

> Down from His glory,
> Ever living story,
> My God and Savior came,
> And Jesus was His name.
>
> . . . .
>
> Without reluctance,
> Flesh and blood His substance,
> He took the form of man,
> Revealed the hidden plan.
>
> . . . .
>
> —WILLIAM E. BOOTH-CLIBBORN

Once a little boy stepped on an anthill destroying many of the ants and sending others frantically running. When he saw their panic, he told his father, "I do wish I could go down there and tell them how sorry I am." "Son," his father said, "the only way you could do that would be to become an ant just like them and speak to them in their language, for only then could they understand." Something like that is what has happened to us —God became a man to tell us that He loves us and has provided for our redemption.

We must remember that when the Word became flesh on that first Christmas morning, He did not begin then to exist. He simply stepped into the empirical realm at that juncture of history. He had always been the great I AM (John 8:58), but for thirty-three years He lived in human flesh, showing us how God wants men to live. As the living Word, He was acting out the life of God, for in the mystery of the Incarnation He lost none of His divinity in assuming the role of humanity.

The verb *was made* in this verse does not involve the idea of losing what a person or thing is originally with the adding of something else. When Lot's wife looked back, she became a pillar of salt (Gen. 19:26). This is a different concept, for after she became a pillar of salt, she ceased to be what she had been—a living person. But Christ maintained what He was and added thereto. He was still just as much God when He was God in the flesh.

Agnostic philosophers said that the gods, if they existed at all, would never touch the sinful flesh of men. But the Bible says that is precisely what Christ did. The Word became flesh, he took on Him a human body, thus identifying Himself with us, yet without sin. Nothing of His deity was sacrificed in becoming a man, nor was his manhood sacrificed or distorted by His being God. He willingly limited Himself to the limitations of a human mind and body for thirty-three years. He was hungry, He wept, He hurt, He was alone, lonely, cold, He wept real tears and shed real blood for sin. Not for one moment was He sinful in His life, yet for six hours on the cross, God made Him "to be sin for us, who knew no sin" (2 Cor. 5:21). In some mysterious way, in an experience the world may never understand, God laid on His own Son the iniquity of us all (Isa. 53:6), and He became sin for us. Jesus Christ was the perfect sacrifice for sin because He had lived in a fleshly body and a human nature which was capable of sin, yet He was without sin.

In his book *The Imperial Animal,* Lionel Tiger sug-

gests that scientists will one day isolate the sin cell in
man. When that happens the human race will have no
further problems and the theologians will be out of business. Mr. Tiger is wrong, for sin does not live in the
flesh-and-blood cells of a person. It is a principle within
his heart, a power to which he yields, giving the flesh
the occasion to sin. Jesus never yielded. The rest of us
respond to the temptations that come from within our
minds and hearts, working out those desires through our
bodies, our human flesh.

The Word not only became flesh, says John, but the
Word "dwelt among us." The Greek verb translated
"dwelt" literally means "to tent, to pitch a tent," and
therefore, "to lodge." It has a temporary aspect about it.
Jesus temporarily took up residence with us, tabernacling right here in the midst of us. For thirty-three years,
God moved in and lived right here with us, understanding, bleeding, loving, living, agonizing, hurting, caring,
and dying.

God was one of us for thirty-three years. In the past
God had often seemed to be some abstraction somewhere
out there in eternity, unapproachable, intangible, un-
knowable, though at times he had come close to man.
Adam walked with God before he fell into sin. But then
men fell away from God and His revelation, and com-
munication with God was spasmodic. Moses found a
place where God seemed always to be and knew that every
time he needed to talk with God he could go to the
mountain and find God there. Then one day God gave
him directions for building a beautiful tabernacle out
of wood and skin which would be symbolic of His presence in the middle of the Israelites' camp. Once a year
the high priest could go into the presence of God in the

holy of holies in the tabernacle. But when Jesus Christ came down from heaven and pitched His tent right in our midst, God became one of us to share our problems, to be seen, touched, and felt (1 John 1:1). The Word was made flesh to tabernacle among us, to dwell among us. And now, through the Holy Spirit He is tabernacled within the heart of the believer.

What a glorious truth! "The Word was made flesh and dwelt among us" and dwells still in the hearts of all who by faith know Him.

15. We Beheld His Glory

"And the Word was made flesh, and dwelt among us, (and we beheld His glory, the glory as of the only begotten of the Father,) full of grace and truth" (John 1:14).

JOHN WAS OLD when he wrote this passage of Scripture. He seems to look back to earlier years with sweetness and wonder at his experiences with Jesus and comments, "We beheld His glory." Let us examine three important truths about that glory.

First, what was it that John beheld? The word *beheld* in Greek means both to see with the physical eyes and to do more than that—to see with spiritual insight, to perceive with spiritual perception.

Men have always sensed that mysterious something special about Jesus, aware that there is more than that which first meets the physical eye. Nicodemus met the Lord Jesus. He watched him from the edge of the crowd and sensed that there was that about Him which was different, something he could not explain. One night he could stand it no longer and came to Jesus face to face. He came at night because he was in too big a hurry, too eager to know, and could not wait until the next day. "Master," he burst out, "we know that you are a teacher come from God. I have read, I have studied, I have examined all the great prophets, I have studied the teachings of the rabbis. Yet, you are different. I know you must be from God" (see John 3:1-2).

The Roman centurion, a professional soldier, had seen men die by the hundreds, cursing and blaspheming the Roman Empire. But not one word of profanity fell from the lips of the dying Savior. Only His prayer "Father, forgive them; for they know not what they do" (Luke 23:34). And when the bowels of the earth began to rumble, the heavens blackened, the lightning flashed, the rocks split and the graves opened, the hardened Roman soldier fell to his knees and cried, "Truly this was the Son of God!" (Matt. 27:54).

The saints through the centuries who have loved Jesus, have lived and gladly died for Him, have touched His hands, looked in His eyes, beheld His glory, with the eyes of faith. They have known that this was no ordinary man, for no man is ever again the same who pauses long enough to behold His glory.

John's second word is that Christ's glory was an inherent glory. It belonged to Him by right, it was His personal glory. At His birth the angels sang, "Glory to God in the highest, and on earth peace, good will toward men," because the presence and glory of God had become tabernacled among the sons of men. At Jesus' transfiguration, Peter, James and John saw His glory shine out plainly (Luke 9:28-32). Jesus Himself talked about the glory He had with His Father before the world was (John 17:5). This glory He has given to us who believe in Him (John 17:22). So the writer of Acts records that as Stephen was being stoned for his faith, he looked into the face of the Savior who was standing to receive His own, and beheld the glory of God and Jesus (Acts 7:55–56). And therefore the church will one day be presented to Jesus as "a glorious church, not having spot, or wrinkle" (Eph. 5:27), for it is washed in His blood.

The Greek word for *glory* is *doxa,* which is the root of our word *doxology,* meaning to give glory, to give praise to God. *Glory* is a difficult word to comprehend fully because it contains a foreshadow, a preview, a touch, just a taste of that which is truly unspeakable and inexpressible. Jesus was the express image of God and the glory of the Glorious One was innately His.

Third, let us raise the question, in what way did John behold His glory? There is, of course, the glory of His person. For that is the genius of Christianity. It is all wrapped up in the person of Jesus Christ.

> The name of Jesus is so sweet,
> I love its music to repeat;
> It makes my joys full and complete,
> The precious name of Jesus.
> W. C. MARTIN

> All hail the power of Jesus' name
> Let angels prostrate fall.
> Bring forth the royal diadem
> And crown Him Lord of all.
> —EDWARD PERRONET

The Bible says that God has exalted Jesus so that "at the name of Jesus every knee should bow . . . and that every tongue should confess that Jesus Christ is Lord, to the glory of God" (Phil. 2:9–11).

Further, John and the disciples beheld his glory in His humility, as do we. Throughout the centuries, emperors and kings have ridden into conquered cities with their courts and courtiers, their entrance fraught with pomp and ceremony. But not so with Jesus. He was too busy talking to the poor blind men, or the small Zacchaeuses up a tree to be counting noses in the crowd. He was too concerned with the feelings of a father and the sufferings of a sick child to worry about the multitudes who would crown Him a physical king. He always turned aside to weep over a grave, to feed the poor, to care for the hungry, to lift the fallen, to heal the brokenhearted, to defend the defenseless. John is saying, I think, that we beheld the glory of His pity, His passion, and His love.

If the president, or the queen of England, or a great author or scholar should walk into a room, we would stand in honor. If Jesus Christ should walk into the room, we would kneel in worship. When a great man comes to a town, he is presented with bouquets of beautiful flowers. When Jesus Christ came into the world, it was into the muck and mire of sinful flesh to save the world. And never do we more exemplify the life of our Lord, than when we give ourselves to the lifting of fallen humanity and spreading the sunshine of His love into the dismal night of darkness, the night of a sinful world.

There is more one could say. John certainly beheld Jesus' glory in His miracles. "This beginning of miracles did Jesus in Cana of Galilee," John tells us of the water turned to wine, "and manifested forth his glory; and his disciples believed on him" (John 2:11). There was the glory of Jesus' life (John 12:27–28), the glory of his death (Gal. 6:14), the glory of His resurrection (Phil. 2:9–11; Heb. 2:7–9), and there will be the glory of His returning (1 Pet. 1:7; Matt. 24:30–31).

And what shall we say of the glory of His final victory? Let us all take heart. We may lose a battle along the way, but we are not going to lose the war. We are on the winning side. The atheist, the agnostic, the infidel, the pervert, the prostitute, the purveyor of flesh, the profligate shall not have the last say. The last chapter of history shall be written by the King of kings. The kingdoms of this world shall "become the kingdoms of our Lord and of his Christ; and he shall reign for ever and ever" (Rev. 11:15).

Often I am asked what heaven is going to be like. There is much I do not know about heaven. But one thing is certain; heaven is going to be filled with the praise of God. And two of the words we shall sing and say the most are "Hallelujah" and "Glory!" Glory to the Lamb! "To God be the glory, great things He hath done." We can all with John burst forth in adulation of unbounded praise and say, "We beheld His glory."

16. The Only Begotten Son

"And the Word was made flesh, and dwelt among us, (and we beheld his glory, the glory as of the only begotten of the Father,) full of grace and truth" (John 1:14).

To THIS POINT the emphasis of John's prologue has been upon the gift—the Son. Now, for a moment, John draws our attention to the giver of the gift—the Father. Note first *what* He gave.

God gave us His "only begotten" Son. The expression "only begotten" translates the Greek *monogenēs*—*mono* meaning "only" and *genēs* (related to the root of *genesis*) meaning "descendant," "offspring." The related verb *gennaō* means to beget, to become the father of, to bring forth or produce. It is used in Matthew's genealogy, of the lineage of Jesus: Abraham begat Isaac . . . etc. There it refers to physical birth and begetting. Jesus is God's only begotten Son. Here the emphasis is on the *only*. Jesus is God's unique Son—God has no other sons or daughters begotten in the same way. We by faith in that Son, may *become* sons and daughters, but He is the *begotten* Son, and there is a difference. Only one time did the Father perform the divine chemistry of birth in the miraculous experience of the virgin conception. But even more than that—from all eternity Jesus was the only Son of the Father. He has always been God's Son.

The term *begotten* is an endearing one more than a biological one. It is a term of affection more than a term of genetics. We, through God's grace, are adopted into His family when we believe on Jesus Christ. We are His children—we *become* His sons and daughters. Jesus is the *begotten* Son. The term *begotten* also emphasizes uniqueness rather than generation. Jesus Christ is the only one of His kind.

Second, how was this Son begotten in the flesh? The Bible records that there are four ways in which God brings human life into the world. First, He created human life without ancestry—that is, without either man or woman—when He created Adam. Second, He creates life from both man and woman in the process of normal reproduction. Third, He created life from man without woman, as in the creation of Eve from Adam's rib. And, fourth, showing that He is indeed God and can create life by any and every method, He now creates the birth of His Son by woman without man. In each case, a particular method of birth is created for a particular purpose. Each is unique.

The virgin birth of Jesus Christ, the birth of the Word made flesh—God creating life from woman without man—is the touchstone of the Christian gospel and bespeaks the deity of Jesus Christ as the incarnation of God. You can believe or disbelieve the Genesis account of creation and still be saved. You can believe or disbelieve the story of the crossing of the Red Sea and still be saved. But I doubt seriously that you can disbelieve in the Word become flesh, in the incarnate virgin-born Son of God—that Jesus Christ is God—and be a Christian.

On it hinges all of the Christian gospel. It is critical. It is not any light-hearted, trivial matter. A Savior that is not totally God is a bridge too short on the other end. The incarnation of God in Christ, the deity of the Word, the idea of God becoming flesh is so important that he who denies it, John says in his epistles, is of the spirit of antichrist (1 John 2:22–23; 4:2–3, 9).

Jesus Himself claimed the prerogatives of God. When the Jews looked for a sign, He said, "Destroy this temple," speaking of His own body, "and in three days I will raise it up" (John 2:19, 21). Notice that He did not say, "God will raise it up again," but rather, "I will raise it up again." For He Himself was God.

He exhibited the characteristics of God. At the feast of the Passover, "many believed in his name, when they saw the miracles which he did. But Jesus did not commit himself unto them, because he knew all men" (John 2:23–24). He did not believe in them, for they had believed for the wrong reasons. They had believed only because of the miracles that He performed, not because of who He was. He knew why they believed, for He was God and could read their hearts. "He knew what was in all men," says John. They did not believe in His deity. They believed Him to be a wonder-worker, a magician, a performer––but not God. They rejected His deity. They would not believe that God, not Joseph, was His Father.

The last question is this: Why did God give His only begotten Son? For one thing, He gave because it is His nature to give. He gave because He is a benevolent God. He just cannot keep from giving. While man is ill and evil, God is holy and good. While man is selfish, God is selfless. While man seeks his own good, God seeks the good of others. While man is filled with hate, God is filled with love. While man keeps, God gives, for it is His nature.

"For God so loved the world that he gave . . ."—He gave because He must. He gave because He could do nothing else. He has always given. In Genesis He gave life. In Exodus He gave the people favor (Exod. 3:21). In Joshua He gave them all the land. In Judges He gave the people their inheritance. In Chronicles He gave them rest (2 Chron. 14:6). In the Psalms He gives strength and help (Ps. 29:11, 60:11, 108:12). To Saul He gave another heart. To Solomon He gave wisdom (1 Kings 4:29; 5:12). To David He gave the kingdom of Israel (2 Sam. 7). To Hezekiah He gave a sign (Isa. 38). To Job He gave twice as much as he had before (Job 42:10). To Israel He gave a Savior. To those that received the Savior He gives the power to become the sons of God. To the disciples He gave power over unclean spirits (Matt. 10:1; Luke 9:1). To the hungry He gave bread from heaven (John 6:47–58). To Paul He gave strength in weakness (2 Cor. 12:9). To the church He gives gifts of ministry (Rom. 12:3–8; 1 Cor. 12; Eph. 4:1–16). For the church He gave Himself. In John He gave life and light and a witness and grace. In Timothy He gave Himself a ransom for all (1 Tim. 2:6). In Galatians He gave Himself for our sins (Gal. 1:4). In Ephesians He gave gifts unto men (Eph. 4:8).

Since He gave His only begotten Son, not sparing Him, but delivering Him up "for us all, how shall he not with him also freely give us all things?" (Rom. 8:32). It is the nature of God to give.

Since it is God's nature to give the best, He demands the best. For "to whom much is given, of him will much be required" (Luke 12:48, RSV).

He commanded the Israelites to bring the best of their flocks and produce for a sacrifice (Num. 18:11–14). Everything offered had to be without blemish (Lev. 22: 18–25). He asked them for an offering of precious metals and fine cloth and stones for the Tabernacle (Exod. 25:1–8; 35:1–9). God does not want the leftovers of our service, our possessions, or our love. He wants ourselves —all our love—the offering that hurts (Luke 21:1–4; 10:27; 2 Cor. 8:1–5). We are to give as God has prospered us, the first of our offering on the first day of the week (1 Cor. 16:1–2; 2 Cor. 9:6–12). He wants the first place in our lives.

One last word: God gave the gift, the gift of His only begotten Son, the best gift, the greatest gift, and He gave it *only once* because once was all that was necessary. In Jesus Christ dwells all the fullness of the Godhead bodily, and therefore He was able to be the divine propitiation for the sins of the whole world (1 John 2:2). His sacrifice of Himself was sufficient, because He was perfect and unblemished. He did not have to offer a sacrifice for His own sins (Heb. 7:24–28). All the law was satisfied in the perfect gift of God's Son. And He who clings to that Rock of Ages will need cling to no other thing because there was in Jesus all that God requires.

In the sixth chapter of Hebrews, the writer presents a hypothetical case of a person falling away from Christian faith and experience. It would be impossible to renew such a person again because it is as though they are making Jesus come from heaven again and are making Him die again on the cross (Heb. 6:4–6). But that will never be done again, the writer says in chapter 9 (vv. 25–28). Jesus virgin born again? Tempted again? Tested again? Dying again? Raised again? Never! No, no a thousand times no! Never will it be again. Never again will He be put to an open shame again. In that complete and perfect gift, God provided all that men would need!

The writer of Hebrews goes on to say, "The law having a shadow of good things to come, and not the very image of the things, can never with those sacrifices which they offered year by year continually make the comers thereunto perfect" (Heb. 10:1). The Old Testament sacrifices were incomplete. In the law there was to be a perpetual coming, a perpetual cleansing. But Jesus did not have to suffer often. He died once for all, and He has forever sat down at the right hand of the Father. The writer to the Hebrews says that by God's will "we are sanctified through the offering of the body of Jesus Christ" (Heb. 10:10). Where every priest in the Old Testament economy had to offer the same sacrifices daily, which could never take away sins, Jesus, "after he had offered one sacrifice for sins for ever, sat down on the right hand of God" (Heb. 10:11–12). Jesus sat down because the work was finished; it was completed. That one gift was given once for all, one time and for all men. It was a perfect gift, a complete gift, and a final one. What Jesus Christ has done, He has done forever. What God establishes, He establishes forever.

In Genesis, Abraham's seed was promised inheritance forever (Gen. 13:15). In Exodus, God established His name forever as Jehovah (Jahweh, Exod. 3:15). In Leviticus, God established the everlasting necessity of atonement (Lev. 16:34). In Numbers, God established the right of the priests to be supported by the people (Num. 19:19, etc.). In Deuteronomy the things revealed of God are forever given to us (Deut. 29:29). In Joshua, we are to fear the Lord forever (Josh. 4:24). In 1 Chronicles, the Lord God is blessed forever (1 Chron. 29:10). In 2 Chronicles God's mercy endures forever (2 Chron. 5:13; 7:3). In Psalms, the Lord shall endure forever, He is King forever, and His throne is forever (Ps. 9:7; 10:16; 45:6). David said, "I will dwell in the house of the Lord for ever," "I will bless thy name for ever," and God "ruleth by his power for ever" (Pss. 23:6; 145:1, 2; 66:7). Isaiah calls us to trust in the Lord forever (Isa. 26:4), because His word will stand forever (Isa. 40:8). In Jeremiah His children are to fear God forever (Jer. 32:39). In Ezekiel God says He will dwell in the midst of His children forever (Ezek. 37:9). In Daniel God's kingdom shall stand forever (Dan. 2:44).

In Matthew, "the kingdom, and the power, and the glory" are God's forever (Matt. 6:13). In Luke, Jesus Christ "shall reign over the house of Jacob for ever" (Luke 1:33). In John, the Son abides forever (John 8:35). In Romans, the Creator is blessed forever (Rom. 1:25). In Hebrews, Jesus Christ is the same yesterday, today, and forever (Heb. 13:8). In 1 Peter, the word of God lives and abides forever (1 Pet. 1:23). In Revelation, worship is given God who lives for ever and ever (4:9), and Jesus Christ "shall reign for ever and ever" (11:15). The angels ascribe "blessing, and honour, and glory, and power" to God who "sitteth upon the throne, and unto the Lamb for ever and ever" (Rev. 5:13). Jesus Christ "ever liveth to make intercession" for those who come to Him (Heb. 7:25). He is a priest forever, for He died once for all. To Him be praise world without end, for ever and ever. Amen.

17. Full of Grace

"And the Word was made flesh, and dwelt among us, (and we beheld his glory, the glory as of the only begotten of the Father,) full of grace and truth" (John 1:14).

BECAUSE OF one of the main attributes of Jesus Christ, life need never be wearisome—we do not need to be defeated. There is always the second half for weary players in the game of life, because He is full of grace. Life is often like a game. We seem to be defeated and there seems to be no bright tomorrow. Then the touch of heaven comes, the breath of the Master is felt, and we are given another chance. He is, indeed, full of grace.

If the gospel is anything, it is a gospel of grace. It is the gospel of the second chance for hopeless men. It is hate exchanged for love. It is failure turned into victory. It is defeat traded for glorious triumph. It is God revealing love in Christ and saying to fallen mankind, "Life isn't over yet. There is another half to the ball game."

I think that the shortest documentary ever written about the life of Jesus was perhaps the best: He "went about doing good" (Acts 10:38). Where Jesus Christ went, grace and graciousness went.

There are probably more than a hundred definitions

of grace. Grace is unmerited favor. It is imputed righteousness. It is undeserved opportunity. But it is more—
it is life's second chance. Grace is the gift of a Christ who
is not judgmental and vindictive. It is His word "I understand for I, too, suffered, I too was tempted" (Heb.
2:10–11, 17–18). It is Jesus saying, "I know what you
feel, I know what you are going through. I know your
heartache and rejection. Get your chin up. I love you
anyhow. Forget yesterday and get started on today. Do
better next time. Don't stumble again, but if you do I
will be there again. And I will still love you, and still
love you, and still love you."

Life is filled with problems. The story is told of a
psychiatrist called by the police to go to a bridge to talk
a young man out of jumping. After an hour and a half of
talking with the boy and hearing about all his problems,
they both jumped! A London newspaper carried the
story of a man walking up and down the streets of
London with a sign saying, "Let's try to be nice to each
other. After all, we are all having a miserable time of it."
But grace moves into miserable situations and says, "You
don't have to give up. Take courage—there is hope."

One of the hardest problems a preacher is ever called
upon to assist is the matter of divorce. Jesus seems to
give grounds for divorce in the case of adultery (Matt.
5:32; 19:9), but He also says that whoever looks with lust
in his heart has already committed adultery (Matt.
5:28). So the question becomes, what is adultery? Is
homosexuality an adulterous relationship? Is it grounds
for divorce? Is a man who is married to his job and
ignores his family guilty of a betrayal of his commitment
to his wife? It seems to me that a loving Christ is more
concerned about saying to people with marital prob-

lems, "I love you, I forgive you, I understand, I can help," than He is in condemning.

The fulfillment of the law is love (Rom. 13:8–10), and love is grace, and grace if it is anything is the Good News that there is a second half in the game of life. In the eighth chapter of his Gospel, John recounts the story of the woman taken in adultery. Who can ever forget the force of His words when He closes the conversation with, "He that is without sin among you, let him first cast a stone," and the grace of His "Neither do I condemn thee: go, and sin no more" (John 8:7, 11)?

The doctors of the law, the theologians, the Pharisees were so concerned with their sermons and their scriptures and their laws and rules that they forgot about their people, they didn't care about people's hearts and people's hurts. I can imagine that this act of adultery was committed behind closed doors in the secrecy of darkness. I raise the question, then, how did the Pharisees catch her in the act unless they suspected her, laid a trap, sought her out, and caught her? (And what did they do with the man?) They did not stumble into the situation, they went looking for it. They were far more concerned about their theology than about a human heart that was broken and aching.

The disciples wanted to argue with Jesus as to the responsibility of a man's blindness. "Who did sin?" they asked. "This man, or his parents, that he was born blind?" But Jesus was not concerned about their theological question. He wanted to move them from theology to doxology. "Neither hath this man sinned, nor his parents: but that the works of God should be made manifest in him" (John 9:2–3).

Before the crucifixion of Jesus, Peter betrayed Him

with an oath. Satan laughed in glee, and the imps of hell mocked. Peter who had said, "Though all men forsake thee, never will I," had denied his Lord. But somehow beyond his accusers, Peter looked into the piercing eyes of Jesus saying, "Peter, I love you anyhow," and Peter's heart broke (Luke 22:54–62). But it made him a great preacher of grace and forgiveness, for he had been forgiven much by Christ's grace.

Matthew's account of the Calvary experience indicates that both thieves who were crucified with Jesus reviled and taunted Him (Matt. 27:44), but Luke records that one rejected Jesus and one pled for mercy (Luke 23:39–43). The simple fact is that both rejected Jesus in the beginning, but then one repented and only Luke records the repentance. And what did Jesus say to him—"There is no further opportunity for you"? No, not at all. Rather, he whispers quiet peace to the soul of a dying man—"Verily I say unto thee, today shalt thou be with me in paradise." Jesus is indeed full of grace.

It is told of Fritz Kreisler, one of the greatest violinists of recent decades, that he longed to purchase a greatly admired violin. Time and time again he attempted to make the purchase, but it was not for sale. One day Mr. Kreisler persuaded its owner to allow him to play it. The music that he produced from its strings was enough to charm the angels. It was music which the owner had never dreamed the instrument could create. When Mr. Kreisler laid down the instrument, his eyes were filled with tears at the joy of the violin. The owner said, "Here, take it at no price. If you can make that kind of music on it, you and only you deserve to be its owner."

Just so God's Son, Jesus Christ, can make beautiful music of your life and deserves to be its owner. But men must respond to Him to experience His grace. The woman taken in adultery had to raise her head to see the forgiving face of Jesus. Peter had to look and heed Christ's call. There is no situation in your life too hopeless for His touch, too far gone for His grace, if only you will call on Him while He is near.

18. Full of Truth

"And the Word was made flesh, and dwelt among us, (and we beheld his glory, the glory as of the only begotten of the Father,) full of grace and truth" (John 1:14).

THE COMPILERS of dictionaries, the theologians, the philosophers have all attempted through many centuries to define truth. Pilate asked Jesus simply, "What is truth?" (John 18:38). The Greek word for "truth" is the word *alētheia*. It has the sense of dependability, to be correct and not false. Perhaps the best understanding of truth is to say that truth is *agreement between mind and reality*. It is never easy for us to act out in truth that which we dream within. All of us dream more than we can do and aspire to be more than we are. It is wonderful to dream and it is important to dream, but seldom is the gap bridged between what we dream and what we accomplish.

The distance from desire to reality can be a million miles. But there was one time in all of the world when someone was able to fulfill completely the expression of a desire. That someone was Jesus Christ. He was a true expression of the mind and heart of God in terms that man could comprehend. God is invisible spirit, but in

Jesus Christ He became a visible person. If Jesus Christ had failed in one point to be the perfect expression of all that God was and felt, He could not justly bear the name Truth. But He failed not a single time. He perfectly lived everything that the Father wanted to say about Himself. Thus, He is the Truth. Jesus said of Himself, "I am the way, the truth, and the life" (John 14:6). Into a world filled with confusion and misdirection He came to say, "I am the way." In a world filled with confusion, perplexity and falsities He came to say, "I am the truth." In a world filled with death and darkness, He came to say, "I am the life."

Jesus is the truth about God. He is the thought made reality. And when the Truth tells you the truth about the Truth, you've got the truth! Jesus was true man and true God. He stood before Pilate's judgment and was asked, "What is truth?" There are those who think that Pilate asked that in jest. I doubt it. Pilate had too much at stake. When he found Jesus innocent he risked his whole future. He gambled with his entire political future. Pilate was in earnest. And yet, when he asked Jesus, "What is truth?" Jesus looked at him in solemn silence and uttered not a word. Why? Because Jesus was saying to him by His very silence, "Pilate, you have seen the truth. Truth is not merely what is spoken, truth is agreement between mind and reality. You have seen the mind of God acted out in reality. You have seen Me. You have examined Me. You have seen the truth. What need have you that I speak to you of truth? When you have seen Me, you have seen it! If you can stand here and look at the truth and not comprehend the truth, you will never understand it by my telling you."

When Jesus said, "Ye shall know the truth, and the

truth shall make you free" (John 8:32), He spoke not of ideas or philosophies but of Himself. He was saying, "When you know Me you shall be free, for I am the Truth." Jesus is the truth about God. He is the truth about love, the truth about life, the truth about forgiveness, the truth about grace.

"And the Word was made flesh, and dwelt among us, (and we beheld his glory, the glory as of the only begotten of the Father,) full of grace and truth."

19. He Is Greater

"John bare witness of him, and cried, saying, This was he of whom I spake, He that cometh after me is preferred before me: for he was before me" (John 1:15).

To THE JEWS, precedence of birth was of great importance. It mattered greatly to them who was the eldest in a family or group. John the Baptist was keenly aware that because of his geographical proximity and the proximity of his age to Jesus, there was the possibility that people would miss Christ and exalt him. He was older than Jesus by about six months (Luke 1:36). But John was concerned that people understand that the servant is not greater than his lord. Jesus was before all things. Jesus was eternal.

The expression, "preferred before" which John uses in reference to Christ is a Greek phrase referring to rank or importance. "He ranks before me—ahead of me—even though His ministry started after mine, because He existed long before I did." John the Baptist and his peers were very class conscious. John is saying, "Here comes a man of real rank. He deserves to make the grand entry, not I. The King of kings, the President of the universe, has something to say!"

The saying is that gentlemen prefer blondes. But, let it be said with far greater truth that true gentlemen prefer Christ above anything else! He is the preferred stock in the company of the eternal. He is no common stock. He does not fluctuate with the whims of the stock market. Jesus is the same yesterday, today, and forever. They talk about a certain insurance company that is built on the rock. *Jesus* is the rock! He never loses value. He never fails. He never goes bankrupt. The company of believers does eternal business with heaven, where the Father is the President, the Holy Spirit is Chairman of the Board and the Son is the majority stockholder. He changes not. His work is impeccable, His workings indescribable, par value, par excellence.

John the Baptist is saying, "Don't look at me. Look at Him. He is preferred before me. I am a man of failures and shortcomings like yourself. But He who comes after me is God in a man's body and He is perfect. There is no weakness in Him. There is no failure in Him, and though He comes after me, yet He is preferred before me, for He was before me."

For something to be preferred before another simply means that it is regarded with higher esteem and is the greater. As God is greater than man, so are His provisions greater than our needs. Exodus says that He is greater than all gods (Exod. 18:11). In Job, He is greater than man (Job 33:12). Isaiah says that God has no equal (Isa. 40:25), and He will not give His glory to another (Isa. 42:8). John's Gospel was written to a people filled with tradition and pride. To them, Jesus is introduced as greater than Abraham, greater than Jacob (John 8:53; 4:12). He told the Jews that He was greater than the Temple, greater than Jonah, greater than Solomon

(Matt. 12:6, 41, 42). In the tenth chapter of John, Jesus sums it all up with the declaration, "My Father . . . is greater than all" (10:29). So let us consider seven great attributes of this preferred Christ.

1. His grace is greater than our sins. The old-time preachers used to preach on five things God does not know—God does not know a man that He does not love, a sin He does not hate, a sinner He cannot save, a pardoned transgression that He cannot forget, and a sin that He cannot forgive. God promises to hide our sins behind us as far as the east is from the west (Ps. 103:12). He promises to remember them against us no more (Jer. 31:34; cf. Isa. 43:25). Through Christ God promises, "Him that cometh to me I will in no wise cast out" (John 6:37). Little wonder John Newton's beloved hymn has become the theme of the redeemed:

> Amazing Grace, how sweet the sound,
> That saved a wretch like me.
> I once was lost, but now I'm found,
> Was blind, but now I see.

Jesus Christ does not know a sin that He cannot forgive, nor a forgiven sin He cannot forget. For what He forgives He forgets. He is a friend like unto no other. He is a preferred friend above all. His grace is greater than our sins.

2. His strength is greater than our temptation. Life in reality can be boiled down to one important question, "Will I do right? Will I be true to the right?" And when that commitment is firmly made, you have the confident assurance that through Him, there is no temptation that can overtake us but that our God is able to deliver us

from it. Oh, glorious truth, God will always with the temptation provide a way of escape (1 Cor. 10:13). If we will but ask, He will give us wisdom and strength (James 1:5; 4:2). He remains faithful, and though we deny Him, He cannot deny Himself (2 Tim. 2:13). Christ's strength is made perfect in our weakness (2 Cor. 12:9). His grace is greater than our temptation.

3. His peace is greater than our fears. Sigmund Freud said, "Every man has something of which he is afraid." The Bible says that one of the main signs of the end of the world will be that men's hearts will fail them for fear (Luke 21:26). This is the most fear-ridden generation that we have ever known. We are afraid of war, we are afraid of peace. We are afraid of integration and we are afraid of segregation. We are afraid of inflation and we are afraid of recession. Psychologists have categorized scores of fears—ophidiophobia, fear of snakes; acrophobia, the fear of high places; agoraphobia, the fear of open spaces; and even phobophobia, the fear of fear itself.

David's reaction to fear was, "What time I am afraid, I will trust in thee" (Ps. 56:3). In his 23rd Psalm he starts out talking *about* God. God guides and leads. But when the storm clouds come and David approaches the valley of the shadow of death, God becomes his personal God who is right there with him. He is no longer talking only *about* God, he is talking *to* God. Now it is *"thou art with me; thy rod and thy staff they comfort me."* David knew the touch of peace found in the presence of the Savior who is the only hiding place amid the gathering storms of life.

> What a friend we have in Jesus.
> All our sins and griefs to bear.
> What a privilege to carry,

Everything to God in prayer.
Oh, what peace we often forfeit,
Oh, what needless pain we bear.
All because we do not carry,
Everything to God in prayer.
—JOSEPH SCRIVEN

4. His comfort is greater than our sorrow. Through the years I have found a study of people's reactions to funerals to be a more accurate mirror of the philosophies by which they live. "Have another drink," some say. "He wouldn't want you to be sad." "He is not really dead. It's only in your mind," says the denialist. "What is the use of mourning, we all have to die sometime," adds the fatalist. "Go ahead and hit me again, I can take it. Death, you can't hurt me," says the stoic. But for the Christian, death is a strange mixture of joy and sorrow. We sorrow, but not "as others which have no hope" (1 Thess. 4:13). There is an overwhelming sense of ultimate victory and confidence in the truth that Christ "hath done all things well" (Mark 7:37). Our faith in Him will not fail us in our trying hour, when we find that our Christ is good to live by, but better to die by.

5. His blessings are greater than our sacrifices. He tells us to trust Him and try Him, to bring our tithes and offerings into the storehouse and see if He will not give good measure, pressed down, and running over even more than we can contain (Mal. 3:10; Luke 6:38). As good stewards, we need to invite Jesus Christ into our lives as Lord of our finances, so that He can work miracles in our behalf. I challenge you to get into a giving contest with God. You will learn to your joy that no man can outgive God.

6. His reward is greater than our expectations. The

Bible speaks very clearly of the principle of reward for faithfulness to opportunities. Our Lord spoke clearly when He said, "To whom much is given, of him will much be required" (Luke 12:48, RSV). But when we hear the wonder of His blessed "Well done, thou good and faithful servant: thou hast been faithful over a few things, I will make thee ruler over many things: enter thou into the joy of thy Lord" (Matt. 25:21, 23), it will indeed be worth it all! For "eye hath not seen, nor ear heard, neither have entered into the heart of man, the things which God hath prepared for them that love him" (1 Cor. 2:9). If this world, as wonderful as it is, was spoken into existence by the word of His mouth, what is heaven going to be like that He has been working on for two thousand years? For He said, "I go to prepare a place for you" (John 14:2).

7. His patience is greater than our failures. He is a merciful God, "slow to anger, and plenteous in mercy. . . . He hath not dealt with us after our sins; nor rewarded us according to our iniquities" (Ps. 103:8, 10). He is a loving God, a faithful God even to men who are unfaithful to Him. How mercifully does He deal with us! Our loving heavenly Father always stands ready to receive us—to pardon the prodigal. "For as the heaven is high above the earth, so great is his mercy toward them that fear him. . . . Like as a father pitieth his children, so the Lord pitieth them that fear him. For he knoweth our frame; he remembereth that we are dust" (Ps. 103: 11, 13–14).

Years ago a young soldier came home from the war and called his parents from San Francisco to inform them that he would arrive the next day. Toward the end of the conversation, after they recounted the joys of their long anticipated reunion, he asked if he could bring a friend home to stay with him. "Certainly," said the parents. "We would be happy to have your friend." "Mother," said the boy, "my friend has one arm, one eye, and one leg." "Oh, son, I do not know if we can take care of a cripple. He would not be welcome. Don't bring him with you." Immediately the phone clicked on the other end of the line. The days went by and the boy did not come home. Within a few short weeks, a body was identified, a suicide note found, and the parents were informed that their son had committed suicide. Shortly after, the body arrived home. Opening the casket, to their amazement, the parents found the body of their son, with one arm, one leg, and one eye.

God is not like that. He will never reject us, no matter how mutilated óur souls, or how battered we become. He loved us even when we were sinners, and demonstrated that love by having His Son die for us when we were far from whole (Rom. 5:5–8).

How wonderful is Jesus! How wonderful is His patience when we fail, when we are ugly. When we are unlovely and unattractive, He loves us still. Though we fail Him, He cannot fail us. As Charles Wesley has so beautifully written,

> And can it be that I should gain
> An interest in the Saviour's blood?
> Died He for me who caused His pain?
> For me, who Him to death pursued?
> Amazing love! How can it be,
> That then, my God, shouldst die for me?
>
> He left His Father's throne above,
> So free, so infinite His grace,·

Emptied Himself of all but love,
And bled for Adam's helpless race.
'Tis mercy all, immense and free;
For, O my God, it found out me.

His grace is greater than our failure.

20. His Fullness

"And of his fulness have all we received, and grace for grace" (John 1:16).

As HE LOOKS BACK on the life of Jesus, the Apostle John is overwhelmed at what he has received from that life and how it has enriched many lives. The glory of the Word made flesh, His grace and truth, could not be contained in that one Life but radiated out through the whole world. "Of his fulness have all we received."

Three questions must be asked about Christ's fullness. Who may receive it? How is it to be received? What is contained therein?

First, then, who may receive this fullness of Christ? I would be remiss if I did not say that there is a very real sense in which Christ's legacy is to all the world. The cross of our Lord Jesus Christ provides for all mankind a substitute, a ransom, a propitiation, an attraction and an invitation. But there is a limited sense in which some of its provision is for the believer only; only those who respond to the invitation receive salvation, justification, sanctification.

It is obvious that the benefits beyond Christ's cross to all of society are unspeakable. Our educational system, for example, was built on principles established by four original schools in the East: Harvard, Yale, Princeton, and William and Mary, schools which were established to train young men for the ministry. Many see the roots of modern labor unions and child labor laws in the preaching of John Wesley and later D. L. Moody. There are, indeed, far-reaching ramifications of the benefits of His fullness to the world-at-large.

But there are specific benefits to the person who truly believes, who puts his trust in Jesus Christ. Jesus said that "he that believeth on me, the works that I do, shall he do also; and greater works than these shall he do" (John 14:12). Through the technology of the mass media the church today is able to reach far more people than Christ reached. Because of Christ's presence, now everywhere in all believers through the Holy Spirit, there is so much power available to us that we will never exhaust the adequacy of the vastness of His fullness.

Paul declares, "My God shall supply all your need according to his riches in glory by Christ Jesus" (Phil. 4: 19). Everything is promised to the believer: "All things are yours . . . and ye are Christ's" (1 Cor. 2:21, 23). Those who have been quickened by God through faith in Jesus Christ have received gifts so that we might grow up "unto a perfect man, unto the measure of the stature of the fulness of Christ" (Eph. 2:4–9; 4:9–13). We who have received Christ Jesus the Lord are to walk "in Him; rooted and built up in him . . . for in him dwelleth all the fulness of the Godhead bodily. And ye are complete in him" (Col. 2:6–7, 9–10). Little wonder that John wrote, "Of his fulness have all we received."

When he was still a shoe salesman, D. L. Moody heard a preacher say, "The world has yet to see what God can do with one man completely surrendered to His purpose." "I will be that man!" was Moody's response. And we all know how much was accomplished through Moody's ministry. How much fullness there is to be tapped—how much fullness to be experienced by the man who dares to believe.

Our second question is, how is that fullness to be experienced? Jesus said that our doing greater works than His would be because He was going to the Father and would send the Holy Spirit. In the Old Testament era, the Holy Spirit came upon men—like David and Samson —for brief periods of time equipping them for special service. He was not a permanent indweller of the hearts of men. But now, because Jesus has died once for all, and has sat down at the right hand of the Father, He has sent His Holy Spirit to change men's hearts permanently. The Spirit's indwelling presence is permanent. He is in all of us who believe in Christ. He is not a commuter; He does not come and go. He is a permanent inhabitant in the heart of the believer.

The person who wants to experience His fullness must want to be emptied of sin, for to the degree that he is not empty, just to that degree he will not be filled with the Spirit. For the believer to be filled with the Spirit, he must first of all desire to be filled, he must want to be more than anything else in the world.

Hearing a returned missionary telling of the glories of the Spirit-filled life, a very affluent lady said, "Sir, I would give the world to have what you have." "My dear lady," said the missionary, "that is exactly what it cost me." There must be desire to be filled with the Spirit.

To be filled with the Holy Spirit, there must also be confession and honest acknowledgment of sin. There must be agreement with God of sin's wrong. Admission, yes, but also repentance, a godly sorrow which changes the heart and mind and issues in action.

To be filled with the Holy Spirit, there must also be faith. To be filled with the Spirit is to ask in faith, believing. For as God imparts His righteousness to the sinner on the basis of faith, just so, He imparts the gift of the Spirit's fullness to those who believe. "How much more shall your heavenly Father give the Holy Spirit to them that ask him?" Jesus told us (Luke 11:13).

In a sense we have already answered our third question, what is contained in that fullness? The Greek word for fullness suggests that it is an endless supply, an inexhaustible reservoir. John describes the fullness that we have all received as "grace for grace." The literal rendition is grace *upon* grace. Grace upon grace upon grace— an endless, amazing supply of wonderful grace. Grace is both the vehicle of and the motivation for our salvation. Grace caused it in the heart of God; grace made possible the Savior's sacrificial death for us; grace keeps Him loving us though we sin. Indeed, it is grace upon grace upon grace.

Stephen F. Olford tells the following story: A wealthy man had purchased a new Rolls Royce. The salesman delivered him all the information regarding his new purchase except one fact which he greatly desired. He simply wanted to know the horsepower of the new automobile.

"Sir," the salesman replied, "traditionally through many years the Rolls Royce Company has never revealed the horsepower of our product. The horsepower of the Rolls Royce is simply not available."

"But, sir," the customer replied, "I have purchased a

$25,000 automobile. I have a right to know. I demand to know the horsepower of this automobile!"

The salesman sent a telegram to the home company in London stating, "New purchaser of Rolls Royce demands to know the horsepower." The next day the proud owner came again with his attorney demanding the response to his cable. Again the company refused his request, stating that it was the tradition of the company that the horsepower was never revealed. The salesman sent another telegram stating, "Please advise horsepower of Rolls Royce. New owner demands information. Threatens lawsuit."

A second time the purchaser gathered with his at- attorney and a small crowd of friends at the office to receive the cable which finally came in answer to his inquiry. The envelope was opened and the cable, containing one word, was read: "Adequate."

That is what John is saying. For all who receive Jesus Christ there is grace upon grace. Grace is found in Jesus, and to have Him is to experience grace adequate for any eventuality.

21. Law and Grace

"For the law was given by Moses, but grace and truth came by Jesus Christ" (John 1:17).

As JOHN presses toward the climax of his argument in the prologue, he begins to zero in on some specific truths and makes sure that they are steadfast in the minds of his readers. He is writing to Jews, who are proud people, steeped in their tradition of Moses' law. "It is important to remember," he seems to be saying, "that the law is good and necessary. But I want you to understand fully that Christ is the fulfillment of that law, and grace and truth came by Him. Grace is the essence of Christ's coming."

Grace is not simply a good luck charm. It is not a fraternity boy in a talent show promising to do his best by the grace of God, nor is it simply the beautiful grace of a floating swan or a lovely ballet dancer, nor is it simply the inside track in personal relationships between ourselves and people of whom we say, "They are in our good graces."

In a judicial sense, grace means mercy or clemency. Theologically it means unmerited favor. Musically, it is a little note added as an embellishment that is barely noticed or heard. In insurance it is a free period, an extension period tacked on at the end of the date established in the policy. In some churches a bishop is referred to as "your grace," and in Europe a duke is also "your grace." But, it is far more than that to the believer. Paul Tournier, eminent European doctor and writer, says in his book *Guilt and Grace* that God's grace is the essence of Himself.

Years ago, a young boy was trying to cross a swollen river. There was a large crowd on the bank including President Jefferson on horseback. Not knowing who he was, the lad picked out the president and asked him for help across the river. President Jefferson agreed and took the boy across. People later asked the boy how he happened to choose the president, not knowing that it was he. "I just looked across the crowd," said the lad, "and some of them seemed to have a 'no' face and some of them had a 'yes' face." Grace is God with a "yes" face! Grace is God with a smile, with a heart that understands.

John declares that before Christ, the law came through Moses. But, grace came through Jesus. Jesus did not make the law unimportant or erradicate it. On the contrary, he came to fulfill the law, to be above the law, to be more than the law. The dictionary defines *law* as the rule of conduct established and enforced by legislation and authority. In a given community the general condition existing in obedience to such rule is known as the practice and establishment of the law. Biblically speaking, it is the Pentateuch, or the first five books of the Bible and the commands and ceremonies given in them. Specifically, it is the record of God's moral judgment, His requirements of men listed in the Ten Commandments.

Oliver Wendell Holmes said that the law is the mirror

of life. Thomas Aquinas was a bit closer when he said, "Salvation is a supernatural end, unattainable by men, and God, therefore, is obligated to direct men to their sin by the giving of the law." The Apostle Paul says it this way: "The law was our schoolmaster to bring us unto Christ"—our teacher (Gal. 3:24). In the law I see my need. In grace I am given the provision to fulfill the need. In grace the lawgiver has become the father; the judge has become the lover of men's souls, the means of their salvation.

Karl Menninger in his book *The Vital Balance* describes the legalistic believer as one who never made an unsound loan, never voted the liberal cause and never responded to any kind of extravagances. He describes these people as "rigid, chronically unhappy, bitter, insecure, judgmental, vindictive, often sadistic and often suicidal kinds of personalities," and says that they cannot give themselves the pleasure of giving a little, the pleasure of living a little, the pleasure of life, the pleasure of grace.

Into a legalistic web woven by this kind of people God inserted Himself. He made of Himself a human personality and walked across the stage of life for thirty-three years to say that all the law and writings of the prophets are fulfilled in Himself—in the one man whose life was characterized by the greatest four-letter word the world has ever known—*love.* "Love is the fulfilling of the law" (Rom. 13:10), because men filled with God's grace, in deep respect for the law, attempt to fulfill it because they want to, because their hearts have been changed. The law said "Thou shalt not commit adultery," "Thou shalt not steal," "Thou shalt not kill." Jesus came and said adultery is in the heart, stealing is a desire, and to hate is to murder. "Love your enemies, . . . do good to them that hate you," He said. "Pray for them which despitefully use you" (Matt. 5:21–30, 44). Do not speak ill of them or hate them. Grace is the thing. Grace is the word, and love is the reason and the expression. Christ is the grace, the symbol of love.

Moses' law was the authority given by God. Through grace, Christ was His own authority. Moses was a faithful servant, but only a servant. Jesus was a faithful servant, but more than a servant—He was and is the Son (cf. Heb. 3:1–6). Moses was a bearer of revelation. Jesus was Himself the revelation. Moses' law pronounced the curse; Jesus' grace pronounced the blessing. Moses' law dwelt in a thick cloud. Jesus' grace came in glorious light for all to see. Moses' saw sent plagues for punishment. Jesus' grace sent miracles for mercy. Moses' miracles were a national calamity. Jesus' grace is a national blessing. Moses' miracles were destructive. Jesus' miracles were remedial. The law of Moses enslaved. The grace of Jesus set free. The law of Moses induced guilt. The grace of Jesus took it away.

When Jesus Christ came to the banks of the Jordan and John the Baptist cried, "Behold, the Lamb of God which taketh away the sin of the world," John pointed to the imminent moment when the systems and ceremonies and services of the law would be consummated in reality when the Lamb of God would be offered once for all for the sins of the whole world. Under the law, the penitent must come to the right lamb, the right priest, the right altar, on the right day and in the right way. But Jesus Christ through grace is the consummation of all that, the fulfillment of the law. He is both the Lamb and the priest, and no further sacrifice for sin need be offered by saint or sinner.

In Hebrews 2:9 the writer declares, "But we see Jesus, who was made a little lower than the angels for the suffering of death, crowned with glory and honour; that he by the grace of God should taste death for every man." The expression "a little lower" means literally a little while lower. When was Jesus made for a little while lower than the angels? In His death on the cross. He was not lower than the angels when He became a man, for the human kingdom is above the angelic kingdom for two reasons. First, because God made man not angels in His own image. And, second, because God provided for the redemption of fallen man, but made no such provision for fallen angels. The only time that Jesus was made a little lower than the angels was for one six-hour period when, for a little while, He who had known no sin became sin for us (2 Cor. 5:21).

The law condemns. But Jesus, through His grace, paid the penalty of the law when God made Him sin for us under the curse of the law—*death*. Thank God for grace that is greater than all our sins, for grace which is above the law and beyond the law and the fulfillment of the law. How beautifully, how completely John said it, "For the law was given by Moses, but grace and truth came by Jesus Christ."

Uncle Tom's Cabin tells the story of Eliza, the slave, running for her life toward freedom in the North. As she comes to the Ohio River, expecting to escape across the ice into the northern states, her heart sinks as she sees that the spring thaws have come and the river has begun to break. The bloodhounds of Mr. Haley are barking at her heels, in front of her is the cracking ice, and before her is freedom. She has one chance for safety; to cast herself on the uncertain mercy of the ice and inch her way precariously toward freedom. Dramatically the risk is taken and she is safe.

Like Eliza, we find the hounds of hell have been at our heels—the hounds of the law that condemns. Then Jesus came and muzzled the law by fulfilling it. He did by grace what the law could not do—that is, fulfill the righteousness of the law in us.

I trust that all of us are related to Jesus through His grace. The law cannot save. Ordinances cannot pardon. Only as we trust Jesus Christ through faith can we know the power of His amazing grace. The law came by Moses; but grace, amazing grace, comes by Jesus Christ.

22. *The Invisible God*

"No man hath seen God at any time; the only begotten Son, which is in the bosom of the Father, he hath declared him" (John 1:18).

THE APOSTLE JOHN was a Jesus man. He warned that men must not look too hard at him nor too long at Moses, but ever at the person of the Christ. Verses 1, 4, and 18 of chapter 1 should be tied together with that in mind. In these verses he has said the same thing in almost the same way. Don't forget it, he is telling us. Don't misunderstand it. Don't fail to believe it. Understand that Jesus is the expression of the Father, the declaration of God in human form.

Notice first that God is invisible, that God is a mystery. Of all the mysteries, God is the greatest. Invisible, immortal, invincible, spiritual, eternal, omnipotent, omniscient.

More than anything else, men have wanted to see God, to see what He is like face to face. Adam heard the voice of God while walking in the Garden of Eden, but he did not see God. Moses saw His back, but he did not see God (Exod. 33:18–23). Earlier he had seen His glow in the burning bush, but he had not seen God (Exod.

3:2–4). Belshazzar saw the finger writing upon the wall, but he did not see God (Dan. 5:5). Ezekiel saw the four great cherubim of God moving in glory, but he did not see God (Ezek. 1). Paul was blinded for three days by the glory of Christ's presence, but he did not see God. John, exiled on the Isle of Patmos, saw the great city of God coming down, but he did not see God. The Bible says that no man has seen God at any time. That is, no man has ever seen the Father. Jesus, the only begotten Son of God, shows us what God is like. Shadrach, Meshach and Abednego were cast into the fiery furnace by King Nebuchadnezzar. But when the king looked, there was a fourth man with them like unto the Son of God. Every Old Testament as well as New Testament revelation of God in visible form was in the person of Jesus Christ. It is absolutely imperative that God remain invisible, because God is spirit.

Because God is Spirit, those who worship Him must do so in spirit and in truth. In the year 54 A.D. the Apostle Paul landed on the shores of idolatrous Greece and directed his gospel assault to the hearts of her mighty philosophers. Within the Agora of Athens, the marketplace between the Acropolis and Mars Hill, he encountered every conceivable kind of statues and altars to gods. There were gods of pity, gods of persuasion, gods of success, and gods of motivation. But even this did not satisfy the hearts of the Athenians. They built altars to their heroes. There were the goddesses Venus, Diana, Minerva; the heroes Cecrops, Thesius, Cadmus, Hercules; the gods Jupiter, Mercury, Apollo—and many more. The people were anxious to worship what they could see and touch. But God is spirit and He is not to be represented by things made by human hands. Paul declared to the

Athenians that the unknown God, the God who made heaven and earth wanted their worship. And He had revealed Himself in human form—in Jesus Christ (Acts 17:16–31).

In the final analysis, everything God has to say about Himself He has said in Jesus Christ (Heb. 1:1–3). Jesus is God. Jesus is all we will ever see of God. When we see the One high and holy, lifted up and His glory filling the corridors of Heaven, the exalted one whom we shall worship and praise throughout all eternity is the Lamb, the Lord Jesus. Jesus Christ is God!

Conclusion

The scriptural admonition is ever "Be ye doers of the word and not hearers only." The record of God to His beloved world is threefold: Christ, the living Word; the Bible, the printed Word; and His body, the church, His post-pentecost visual Word.

Paul added that there is enough of God in the human conscience and in nature to convict man of the reality of God and make man respond to God (Rom. 1, 2). The witness of God is ample. The question then becomes, "What will you do with Jesus who is called the Christ?" Neutral you cannot be. The Master Himself clearly stated, "He that is not with me is against me" (Luke 11:23).

But the ultimate test of every doctrine is that of Scripture validated in the crucible of experience. We need to act on what we know. Throughout my ministry I have met many persons who claimed they wished they were Christians, but who were not. No one has to stay in that state. The invitation is "O taste and see that the Lord is good: blessed is the man that trusteth in him" (Ps. 34:8). Anyone may cry to Him, "Lord, I believe. Help thou mine unbelief."

Let us start where we are and exercise the faith we possess. If we seek Him with all our heart, we will come to know Him. And knowing Him is to have life abundant.

As B. B. McKinney put it so well:

Jesus is standing at your heart's door,
Standing and knocking, He's knocked before;
This is the question you face once more:
What will you do with Jesus?
What will you do with Jesus?
Neutral you cannot be;
Some day your heart will be asking:
"What will He do with me?"